SEASONAL AND HOLIDAY HAPPENINGS

Can · Make · and · Do Books

SEASONAL AND HOLIDAY HAPPENINGS

150 Experiences for Children: Cooking, Arts and Crafts, Science, Bulletin Boards, and Costumes

by Joy Wilt
Terre Watson

Photography by Terry Staus

CREATIVE RESOURCES

Waco, Texas

Contents

III. MONTH BY MONTH HAPPENINGS

Acknowledgments

Seasons and holidays should be an enjoyable and important part of every child's life. We hope that together we can share this excitement with many.

Special thanks are due to our very talented photographer, Terry Staus, and to the children who shared their time and creativity in the photographs for this project—Casey Augulius, Marty and Shelby Free, Allison and Christine Persing, and Brad Grady.

From Terre, personal thanks to her parents, Russell and Melena Edmonston, for all the joy and love they shared in helping her discover the beauty and excitement in seasons and holidays, and to her brother, Bob, and aunt, Dessie Vukanovich, for help in editing and typing; to her husband, Bill, for his concern and enthusiasm for this project and for being such a large part of her holiday spirit.

JOY WILT
TERRE WATSON

Seasonal Happenings

Egg Carton Garden

1. Mix the dirt and planter mix in a bowl and fill each section of the egg carton three-fourths full with the mixture. Water each section so the soil is soaked but not too sloppy. With a toothpick, poke a hole in the center of each section. Place one carrot or radish seed in each hole. Cover with a little dirt.

2. Cover entire surface of egg carton with a piece of plastic wrap and close the lid. Place carton in a warm place. Open every day, lift off plastic, and water the seeds. When seedlings break through dirt, open cover and remove plastic wrap. Keep carton in a light place and water the plants every day.

You will need:

1 plastic egg carton	1 toothpick
8 tablespoons of planter mix	1 package carrot seeds
8 tablespoons of garden dirt	1 package radish seeds
1 bowl	

3. When the seedlings are 1″ tall, they must be transplanted into larger pots. Clean coffee or honey cans may be used. Punch two holes in the bottom of each can. Mix enough planter mix and dirt to fill the can three-fourths full.

4. With an old spoon, make a hole the size of the egg carton section in the center of the can. Carefully lift out the plant and the dirt from one section of the egg carton and push gently into soil in can. Place plants in a sunny location outside and water a little each day. In four to eight weeks the carrots and radishes should be ready to eat.

Pineapple Plant

You will need:

1 *pie pan*
1 *pineapple top*
   Water

Place the pineapple top in pie pan filled with water. Change the water often. Keep the plant in a sunny location indoors. In a few weeks roots will grow from the bottom of the pineapple plant. When the roots are 2″ long, plant the pineapple in the ground.

Hollowed-Out Garden

You will need:

Assortment of root vegetables: carrots, turnips, rutabagas, sweet potatoes, etc.
Toothpicks
String
Water
Knife

Cut away two-thirds of the vegetable from the tip and discard. From the stem end, hollow out the center section and put three toothpicks in the vegetable. Tie strings on the toothpicks and hang, hollow side up, from a curtain rod or a sunny window. Keep center hole filled with water. Stems and leaves will appear in a few weeks.

Avocado Tree

Put four toothpicks into midsection of avocado seed. Place seed, pointed side up, on top of jar opening, supported by the toothpicks. Fill jar with enough water to keep seed submerged. Keep in sunny location and replenish water as it evaporates. In about three weeks, roots will grow from bottom of seed and a stem from the top. When the root is about 3″ long, remove toothpicks and plant seed in ground. (This tree will not yield avocados.)

14

Pie Pan Lawn

You will need:

1 *pie pan*
  Potting soil
  Dirt
  Grass seed
  Water

Mix potting soil and dirt in equal amounts. Fill pie tin half full. Sprinkle grass seed on top of soil. Cover seed with thin layer of potting soil and dirt. Keep in sunny location outdoors and water every day. Grass should begin to appear in a few days.

Dew

You will need:

1 glass
   Water
   Ice cubes

Fill glass with water and ice. Wait a few minutes. Soon water beads will form on outside of glass. The reason: The ice water cooled the glass, which cooled the air around it. Because cold air holds less water vapor than warm air, as the air around the glass was cooled, the vapor condensed into drops of water. Dew is formed in the same way. As the air close to the ground cools off during the night, the water condenses on plant leaves, grass, and other objects on the ground.

Drying Flowers

You will need:

1 cup borax
2 cups oatmeal
1 shoe or gift box
  Fresh flowers

Use fresh, bright-colored flowers with 1″ stems to preserve. In a bowl, mix 1 cup borax and 2 cups oatmeal. Pour half the mixture in a shoe box, place the flowers face down in the box, and cover with the remaining mix. Cover the shoe box and leave at room temperature for three to four weeks before removing from box.

Daisy Crown

1. Cut daisies with stems as long as possible. Lay the first daisy horizontally in front of you with flower to left. Place second daisy at right angles to and behind first daisy. Bend stem of second daisy up and over stem of first daisy, then around its own blossom. Bring second daisy stem alongside first stem. Now place third daisy at right angles to and behind first two stems. Bend this stem up and over stems of first two flowers, then around its own blossom. A paper clip will help keep stems together. Repeat this procedure until the daisy crown is large enough to fit around the head.

You will need: *Scissors*
Paper clips
Fresh daisies, mums, or other fresh flowers (enough
    to go around the head)

2. Cross the first flower of the crown over the end stems. Wrap some short-stemmed daisies over the overlapping ends. Secure with a paper clip, making sure all loose ends are tucked into the crown. The daisy crown is ready to wear.

Incubator

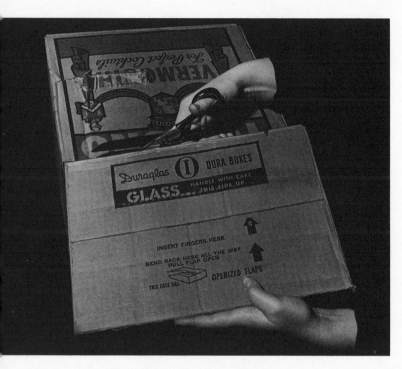

1. Cut top flaps off small box.

2. Place small box on its side. Cut slit from open end to middle of top of this box. Make slit large enough so cord of a single light fixture can slip through it. Put cord in slit and hang bulb inside box. Now place small dish of water, thermometer, and several eggs in bottom of this box.

You will need: 2 *cardboard boxes (one must fit inside other with space left between)*
1 *thermometer*
1 *light bulb and fixture*

1 *small dish of water*
1 *6″ x 6″ square of glass*
Fertile chicken eggs
Newspaper
Knife

3. In bottom of large box, cut a 6″ square window. Tape glass or plexiglass into it for the observation window. Slide small box into large box with open face of small box toward observation window.

4. Pack crumpled newspapers into space between boxes. Maintain temperature at 103° F. at all times for 21 days. Experiment ahead of time with amount of newspaper and size light bulb to maintain proper temperature. Then place eggs into small box, turning them 3 times a day to insure even heating. For proper humidity, be sure there is water in the bowl at all times.

21

Spring Bulletin Board

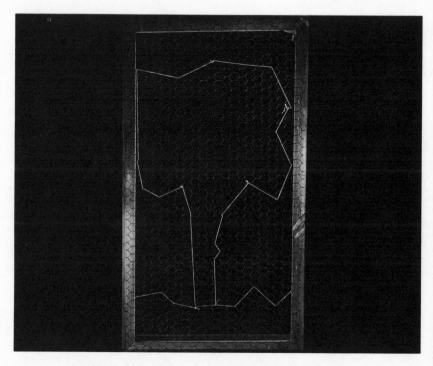

1. Staple the chicken wire to the wood of the bulletin board, or place it on a table while the children work and staple it to the frame after completing step 2. In the chicken wire, string a design of a peach tree, grass, and sky.

You will need: *Chicken wire (enough to cover a bulletin board)*
Tissue paper in varied shades of green, pink, blue, white,
   and brown
Yarn or string

2. Cut the tissue paper in 4″ x 4″ squares.
Push the middle of these squares part
way into the holes of the chicken wire.
Use green for grass and tree leaves;
brown for tree trunk. Use shades of
pink and white for tree blossoms and
blue and white for sky. Continue until
the chicken wire is filled.

Heat Absorption

You will need:

2 tin lids
 Black paint
 White paint
 Lighted electric bulb

Paint one lid white and the other black. Place the lids under the lighted bulb. After a few minutes, feel the lids. Notice that the black lid is much hotter. **Variation:** Cover one test tube in black paper and one in white paper. Fill with water and place in the sun for an hour. Take a temperature reading. The black one should be about 10° higher. The reason: white reflects the light rays which produce heat while black absorbs them.

Heat and Water Evaporation

Place equal amounts of water in each jar. Put one directly in the sun, over a heater, or in another warm place. Put the other in the coolest spot in the room. Observe these for a week. Since warm air holds more moisture than cold air, warm liquids will evaporate faster than cold ones. Water from our oceans, lakes, and rivers evaporates faster on a warm day than on a cold day.

Summer Weather Evaporation

You will need:

1 *small glass jar with a narrow lid*
   Small bowl
   Water

Fill the jar and bowl, each with the same amount of water. Do not cover. Place on a window sill and observe for a week. Since liquids can evaporate only from the surface and there was less water surface in the jar, water evaporation takes place more slowly there than in the bowl with its larger surface. Notice what happens to lakes, especially in hotter months.

Evaporation and Cooling

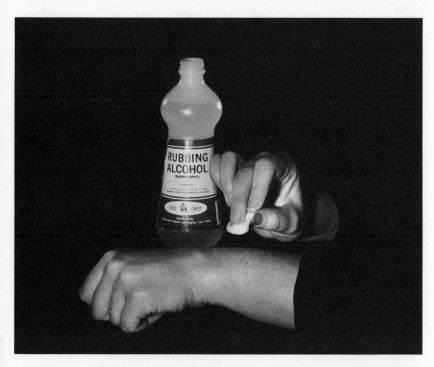

You will need:

Alcohol
Thermometer
Cotton
Cardboard

Dab some alcohol on your arm and feel the spot cool. To find out why, tie a piece of cotton moistened with alcohol on the bulb of the thermometer. Fan with the piece of cardboard and watch the mercury go down. As the alcohol evaporated it cooled the bulb of the thermometer, just as when the alcohol evaporated from your arm it absorbed the heat from your skin and made it feel cool. Evaporation is a cooling process.

Water and Wind

You will need:

Paint brushes
Paint rollers
Buckets or plastic containers
Water

Fill the pails with water. Give each child a paint brush to paint fences, sidewalks, playground equipment, walls, etc., with the water. Have them each paint two objects, fanning one. From which one does the "paint" disappear first? Did the "paint" make the things you painted look different? What happened to the water? How do you know the water is gone? Explain that air currents affect the rate of evaporation. The more wind, the faster evaporation takes place. On a windy day water evaporates rapidly from our oceans, lakes, and rivers.

Walnut Shell Boat

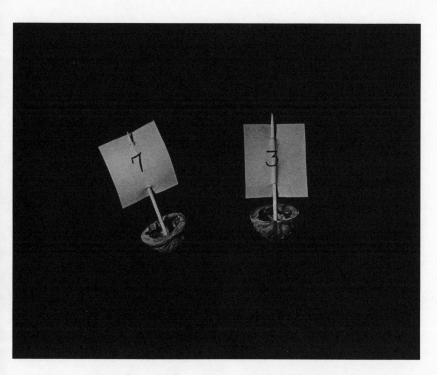

1 *walnut*
2 *toothpicks*
  Nutcracker
  Clay
  Paper
  Scissors

Crack a walnut into perfect halves. Clean out the inside and place a small lump of clay in the middle of each half. Put a toothpick into the lump of clay. Cut two squares of paper 1½″ x 1½″ for the sails. Poke two holes in the sails and weave the toothpick through.

Popsicle Stick Raft

You will need:

12 *Popsicle sticks*
   Waterproof glue

Place two sticks 3″ apart and parallel to each other. Glue the remaining sticks as close as possible on the two sticks. This raft is ready to float in some water. This raft may be dipped into hot paraffin wax to be waterproofed.

Popsicle Stick Paddle Boat

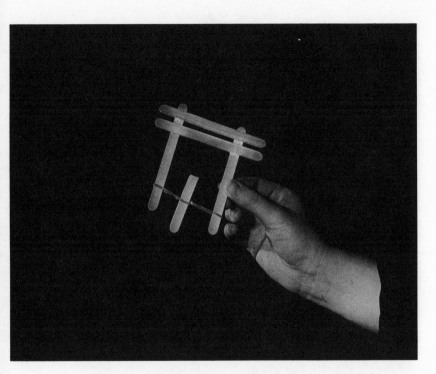

You will need:

4½ Popsicle sticks
1 rubber band
    Waterproof glue or string

Lay two Popsicle sticks 2″ apart and parallel to each other. Connect these at one end with two sticks by gluing. At the open end attach the rubber band and insert the remaining half Popsicle stick through the rubber band. Wind up the propeller and release the boat in water.

Milk Carton Catamaran

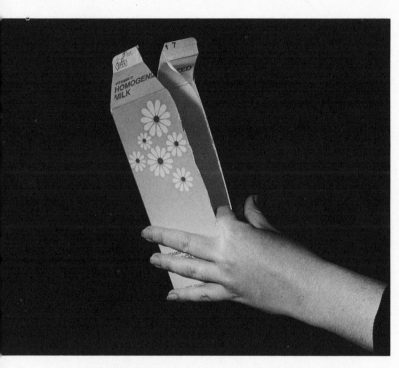

1. Staple pouring spout closed. Place carton as shown. Starting at upper righthand corner of bottom, cut along righthand side to upper righthand corner of top. Stand carton upright and cut diagonally across top from front righthand corner to rear lefthand corner. Lay carton back down and cut diagonally from upper righthand corner of bottom to lower lefthand corner.

2. Open up boat so middle fold line is up and two side fold lines are down. At back of boat, above water line, insert a pencil or a wooden skewer to keep boat open.

You will need: 1   quart or ½-gallon paper milk carton
Scissors
Rubber band
½   Popsicle stick

3. At back of boat in floating position, make a hole on inside of each hull about ¼″ up from bottom. Insert one end of rubber band in each hole, tying a knot on each end inside boat. Place the half Popsicle stick in the rubber band.

4. Wind up the propeller and the catamaran is ready to sail away.

33

Hula Hoop Water Sprinkler

 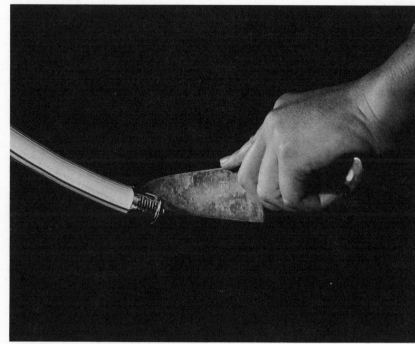

1. Using the ice pick or nail and hammer, poke holes around the Hula Hoop, except for five inches.

2. Cut the Hula Hoop at the midpoint of the five inches. Connect each end of the hoop to the non-threaded ends of the PVC fitting. Use PVC cement to secure them in place.

You will need:

1 *Hula Hoop*	1 *hose washer*
1 *PVC fitting reduced to*	*Ice pick or nail and hammer*
½" female pipe fitting	*Knife*
1 *½" pipe nipple*	*PVC cement*
1 *½" female hose connector*	*Access to outdoor running water*

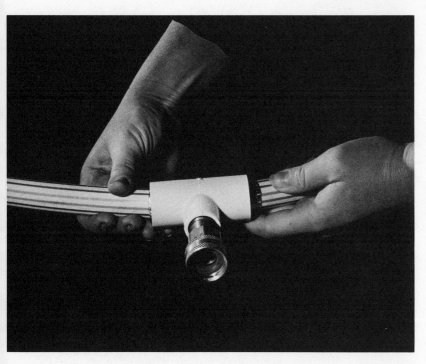

3. Thread the nipple into the threaded end of the PVC fitting. Using the female connector, attach the Hula Hoop sprinkler to a garden hose that is connected to an outdoor water source.

4. The sprinkler is ready to use.

Sun Printing

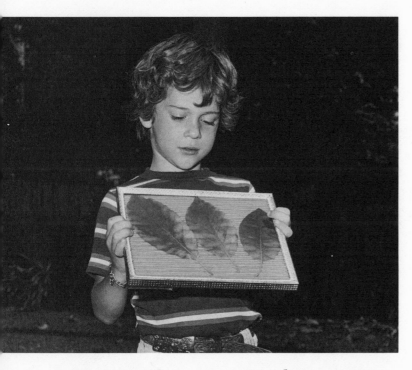

You will need:

Photographic proof paper (or contact printout paper)
Fixer (sodium thiosulfate)
8" x 10" piece of glass
8" x 10" piece of board
Leaves and grasses
Glass dish

Mix ¼ cup fixer to two cups hot water in a glass dish and let it cool. Lay a piece of proof paper on the board; arrange leaves and grasses on top and cover with the piece of glass. Expose to the sun until the paper turns dark purple. This should take about a minute and a half in bright light. Remove the glass and leaves. Place the paper in the fixer for three minutes and rinse it under running water for five min-utes. The paper will turn brown in the fixer. Let the picture dry flat.

Lemon and Peppermint Stick

You will need:

1 *lemon*
1 *peppermint stick*
  Knife

Roll the lemon on a table to break down the inside. Cut a hole in one end of the lemon. Break a small section of the peppermint stick off. Insert inside the lemon and suck. The juice of the lemon and sweetness of the candy will make a perfect combination.

Making Ice Cream

You will need:

1 clean coffee can and lid
1 ice bucket or plastic pail
1 egg
½ cup honey
1 cup milk
½ cup cream
1 teaspoon vanilla
   Salt
   Rock salt
   Crushed ice

In the coffee can, beat the egg and honey. Add the milk, cream, vanilla, and a dash of salt. The can should not be more than half full. Cover the coffee can. Put a layer of ice in the pail and sprinkle a spoonful of rock salt on it (table salt doesn't work as well but can be used). Place the coffee can in the pail on top of the layer of ice. Pack more salt and ice around the sides of the can, up to the top of the can.

Open the can and have the children take turns stirring the mixture around with a big spoon. Allow the can to turn also. It will take 15–30 minutes for the ice cream to freeze to mush. It's ready to eat! If harder ice cream is desired, put the can in the freezer for an hour.

38

Summer Bulletin Board

Have the children draw a picture of their dream vacations on a piece of paper. Mount the pictures on colored construction paper and pin them on the bulletin board. **Variation:** Have the children describe their dream vacations with pictures cut from a magazine and glued onto a piece of paper.

You will need:

Paper
Crayons, paint, or felt-tip markers
Bulletin board

Glycerin Leaves

You will need: *Glycerin (buy at drugstore), small branch of leaves (green or just turning colors), newspaper, hammer, large jar*

1. Place the branch on several layers of newspapers. With the hammer, tap the end of the stem until it is slightly crushed.

2. In the jar, mix one part glycerin to two parts water. Place the pounded end of the branch into the glycerin mixture for 2 weeks. By this time the leaves will be thicker to touch, their color will have changed, and they will not disintegrate or fade.

Clay Leaf Prints

You will need: *Self-drying clay, rolling pin, nail, knife, leaves*

1. Using a rolling pin, flatten a lump of clay.

2. Lay a leaf on the clay and roll over it with the rolling pin. Remove the leaf and let the clay dry. Paint the clay with tempera or acrylic paint if desired.

Laminated Leaves

1. Water down the white glue by adding one part water for every two parts glue. With a paint brush, spread the glue onto a sheet of wax paper. Place the leaves on top and cover with more glue.

2. Place a sheet of white tissue paper on top of the leaves, and remove all wrinkles from the paper. Let the construction dry. Hang the picture on a window.

You will need: White glue   Leaves
                    Wax paper   Water
                    White tissue paper Iron
                    Paint brush

3. For a variation, two pieces of wax paper are needed. Place the leaves on top of one sheet of wax paper and place the other sheet on top of the leaves. Iron the top wax paper to seal.

4. A leaf skeleton may be made by placing a green leaf on top of some newspaper and pounding it with a hair brush. Continue pounding until the center part of the leaf is lacy and the veins are exposed. Iron the leaf between two sheets of wax paper.

Contact Paper Leaf Mobile

You will need: *Clear contact paper, leaves, scissors, string or yarn, plastic coffee can lid*

1. Cut contact paper into squares. Place square of contact paper, sticky side up, on table; then place a leaf on it. Cover with another piece of contact paper and stick the two together. Repeat until there are enough leaves for the mobile.

2. Cut around shape of leaf, leaving ¼" border. Punch hole in top and attach piece of string. Punch holes around top of plastic lid. Thread strings attached to leaves through holes, making sure mobile is balanced. Knot strings in place. Punch two more holes on opposite sides and thread piece of string through holes for handle. Knot strings in place.

44

Cooking a Pumpkin

Note: When buying a pumpkin for cooking make sure it is a "sugar pumpkin" grown especially for eating. Some varieties of pumpkin which are for decorating only will not cook properly.

You will need: *1 sugar pumpkin*
Large pot
Knife
Spoon
Water

Steamer
Cookie sheet
Vegetable oil
Salt

Pumpkin Pulp:

Cut the pumpkin into quarters and remove the strings and seeds completely. Save the seeds. Cut the cleaned pumpkin into pieces and cook in boiling water in a covered pot until soft. Remove the pumpkin from the pan and separate the pulp from the rind. Mash the pulp or put it through a sieve. When the pulp has cooled, use it in the same manner as canned pumpkin. It may also be frozen.

Pumpkin Seeds:

Wash the seeds and get rid of any pumpkin string. Steam the pumpkin seeds first to soften the outside part of the seed. Put the seeds in a steamer and place in a pot with the water level below the steamer. If the seeds get wet, vitamins will be lost. Keep the pot covered and cook for 30 minutes. Add more water if needed. Remove the seeds from the steamer and pat dry with a paper towel. Spread the seeds on a cookie sheet and pour a little oil on top so the seeds are shiny. Stir around and sprinkle with salt. Bake seeds in a 300° oven for 30 minutes or until golden brown and crispy.

Pumpkin Recipes

Pumpkin Cookies

1½ cups brown sugar
½ cup shortening
2 eggs
1¾ cups cooked pumpkin
2¾ cups flour
1 tablespoon baking powder
1 teaspoon cinnamon
½ teaspoon salt
½ teaspoon nutmeg
1 cup raisins
1 cup chopped walnuts
¼ teaspoon ginger (optional)

Mix all ingredients in bowl except for nuts and raisins. Stir until smooth. Add nuts and raisins and mix until blended. Drop by rounded teaspoonful on ungreased cookie sheet. Bake at 400° 12–15 minutes.

Pumpkin Bread

4 eggs
½ cup water
1 cup vegetable oil
1 cup cooked pumpkin
1½ cups molasses
1 cup brown sugar
3 cups whole wheat flour
1½ teaspoons salt
2 teaspoons baking soda
2 teaspoons cinnamon
1 teaspoon nutmeg
½ teaspoon cloves

Preheat oven to 350°. Beat four eggs with mixer until fluffy. Beat in water, vegetable oil, pumpkin, molasses, and brown sugar. Sift flour, salt, baking soda, cinnamon, nutmeg, and cloves together. Add to batter and beat until smooth. Grease two loaf pans and fill each ⅔ full. Bake 45 minutes to an hour. Let bread cool in pans for 15 minutes before removing.

Pumpkin Pie

Crust:
  1½ *cups flour*
  ½ *teaspoon salt*
  1 *tablespoon brown sugar*
  ½ *cup vegetable oil*
  2 *tablespoons milk*

Filling:
  3 *eggs*
  1½ *cups cooked pumpkin*
  ½ *cup molasses*
  ½ *cup brown sugar*
  1½ *teaspoons cinnamon*
  1 *teaspoon of any mixture of these:*
    nutmeg, cloves, ginger, allspice
  ½ *teaspoon salt*
  13 *ounces evaporated milk*
  1 *teaspoon vanilla*

Preheat oven to 400°. **Crust:** Sift flour, salt, and brown sugar into 9″ pie pan. Pour oil and milk over flour, and mix with fork or fingers. After dough is well mixed, pat dough to cover bottom and sides of pie pan. Put in refrigerator until filling is ready. **Filling:** Crack two eggs in a large bowl. Separate yolk of third egg from egg white. Put yolk with other eggs and save white until later. Mix pumpkin, molasses, brown sugar, cinnamon, spices, salt, milk, and vanilla with egg mixture. Stir well with spoon. Remove crust from refrigerator and brush with slightly beaten egg white to prevent crust from getting soggy. Pour filling into crust and bake at 400° for 50–60 minutes. Pie is done when a knife inserted into pumpkin mixture comes out clean. Cool pie before eating.

Making Peanut Butter

You will need:

30 *peanuts, unshelled*
Corn oil
Food grinder or blender
Bowl
Spoon
Crackers

Shell the peanuts, leaving on the brown skins. Place the shelled peanuts in the food grinder and grind them into a bowl. Add enough oil to moisten the mixture to a spreadable consistency. Peanut butter is good to eat on crackers, bread, banana, celery, lettuce, etc.

Autumn Bulletin Board

Draw a trunk and branches on the butcher paper with brown paint. Have the children dip their hands or finger tips only into one of the colors of paint. The children will make hand prints on the tree branches to represent autumn leaves. **Variation:** Instead of using hand prints, cut out leaf shapes and have the children paint the leaves with the mixture of 2 parts salt to 1 part tempera paint. This will give texture to the leaf shape. Pin them on the tree.

You will need:

Butcher paper to cover the bulletin board
Red, yellow, and brown tempera paints
Salt

Fog

You will need:

1 quart bottle or jar
  Ice cubes
  Boiling water
  Piece of large-holed screen
  Piece of black construction paper

Fill the bottle half full with boiling water. Quickly place the screen on top of the bottle and several ice cubes on top of the screen. Hold the black construction paper in back of the bottle and watch fog form in the bottle. Warm air holds more moisture than cold air and warm liquids evaporate faster than cold ones. When the warm air inside the bottle combines with the moist cool air at the top, fog quickly is produced.

50

Rain Machine

You will need:

Soup ladle or large spoon
Kettle
Water

Fill the kettle with water and bring it to a boil. Put the ladle in cold water until it is very cool. Dry off all the water. Holding the ladle by its handle, position the metal bowl of the ladle so it touches the water vapor that is coming from the spout of the kettle. Within a short time, the vapor will condense on the cold metal and drops of water will fall from the ladle. This same kind of process occurs when rain falls. Heat evaporates the water from our oceans, lakes and rivers; this evaporation forms clouds. When the clouds are cooled sufficiently, they become water again and fall back to earth as rain or snow.

Weaving a Neck Scarf

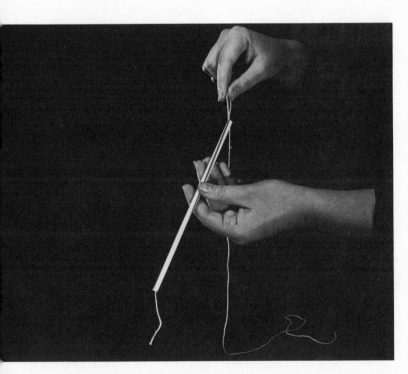

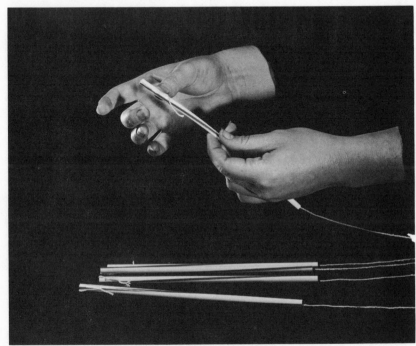

1. Thread a string through each straw.

2. Tape one end of the string to one end of the straw. Repeat this process for the remaining straws; then lay them next to each other and tie the loose ends together.

You will need: 5 *drinking straws*
                          5 *1-yard pieces of string*
                             Tape
                             Thick yarn
                             Scissors

3. Hold the five straws in one hand with the strings down. Keep the straws slightly separated from each other. Knot the end of the yarn to one straw and begin weaving the yarn over, under, over, under, over, under, etc. As the straws fill up with the weaving, push the yarn off the straws onto the strings below.

4. Continue until the strings are filled with weaving. Remove straws and knot the ends of the strings so the weaving cannot slip off. The scarf is ready to wear on those cold winter days.

Soap Flake Snowman

You will need:

2 cups soap flakes
1 cup water
    Small rocks, sticks, leaves, etc.
    Paper
    Small pieces of fabric
    Scissors

Mix the soap flakes and water together. The mixture should be very thick and stiff. Roll the mixture into the shape of a snowman. Decorate him with rocks, sticks, leaves, fabric, paper scraps, etc. The snowman will dry in one day.

Hot Chocolate Recipes

All-American Hot Chocolate

1-oz. jar non-dairy creamer
1-lb. package hot chocolate mix
1-lb. 9-oz. size package of instant milk
1 cup powdered sugar

Mix all the ingredients in an airtight container and store until needed. Add 2–3 heaping teaspoons to a cup of boiling water. Add a peppermint stick, marshmallow or whipped cream for an added treat.

Brazilian Hot Chocolate

2 squares unsweetened chocolate
1 cup water
¼ cup sugar
3 cups milk
1 tablespoon grated orange rind
¼ teaspoon almond extract
   Cinnamon sticks

Melt chocolate and water in top of double boiler over high heat. Stir in sugar and bring to boil over direct heat. Boil for five minutes, stirring constantly. Stir in milk, orange rind, and almond extract. Heat thoroughly before serving. Beat with eggbeater until frothy and serve in cup with cinnamon stick.

Mexican Cocoa

1 tablespoon cocoa
1 tablespoon plus 1 teaspoon of sugar
⅔ cup milk
¼ teaspoon vanilla
   Cinnamon stick
   Marshmallow

Put cocoa and sugar into saucepan. Measure milk in measuring cup. From cup, use one tablespoon milk to mix with cocoa and sugar to form a smooth paste; then add remaining milk and vanilla to cocoa mixture. Stir with cinnamon stick, while heating until warm. Pour into cup and top with marshmallow.

Winter Bulletin Board

Divide the bulletin board into fourths with the yarn and pins. Each fourth will represent a type of winter weather: rain, hail, sleet, or snow. Have the children cut out pictures or draw pictures depicting these types of winter weather. Pin these in corresponding spaces.

You will need:

Yarn
Paper
Crayons
Scissors
Pins
Marking pens

Holiday Happenings

Valentine Mailbox

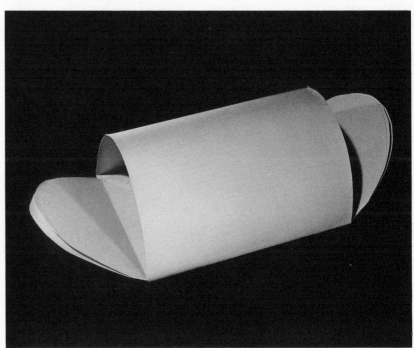

1. On each 12″ side of the 12″ x 18″ paper, make a 1″ fold. Fold the 18″ x 24″ piece of paper in half lengthwise, to measure 9″ x 24″. Then measure in 6″ from each end of the folded paper and fold on these lines.

2. Round the 12″ x 18″ piece of paper and glue the 1″ folded edges to the bottom of the middle section of the 9″ x 24″ piece of paper. Trim the two remaining sides to fit the contour of the top of the mailbox. Tape one end closed; the other will be the door.

You will need:

- 1 18″ x 24″ piece of heavy paper
- 1 12″ x 18″ piece of heavy paper
- 1 1″ x 8″ piece of heavy paper
- 1 4″ x 4″ piece of colored paper
- 1 paper fastener
- Glue
- Tape
- Scissors

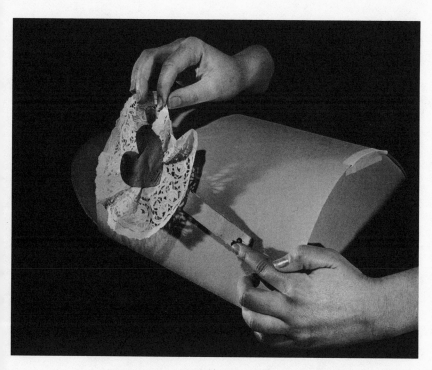

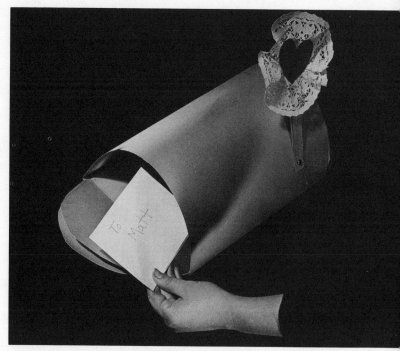

3. To make a flag for the mailbox, glue the 4″ x 4″ piece of paper to the 1″ x 8″ piece of paper. Top with construction paper heart, decorated with doilie if desired. Push the paper fastener through the bottom end of the 1″ x 8″ piece of paper and through the mailbox. Fasten on inside of mailbox.

4. With a piece of tape, make a handle for the mailbox door. The Valentine mailbox is ready to be used to collect Valentine letters.

Folded Heart Envelope

1. On one of the 12″ sides, round off the corners to resemble the top of a heart.

2. Fold the other 12″ side up 7½″.

You will need: *1 12" x 18" piece of red*
                         or pink construction paper
               Stapler
               Ruler
               Scissors

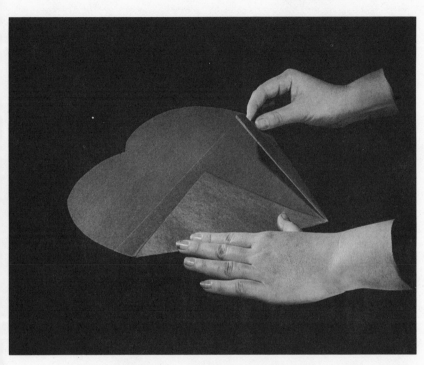

3. Fold the bottom left and right corners to a midpoint, 1" below the top of the folded piece.

4. Fold the 1" strip over the folded corners. Staple it in place. This Valentine envelope is ready to hold Valentines.

Paper Bag Valentine Containers

You will need:

1 paper bag
  Items to decorate the bag
  Glue
  Scissors

Note: All Valentine containers, as well as homemade cards, can be decorated with items such as: paints, crayons, glitter, sequins, foils, doilies, styrofoam, beads, material scraps, tissue paper, ribbon, yarn, egg shells, egg cartons, buttons, lace, rickrack, cotton, toilet paper squares, stickers, adhesive paper etc.

Roll down the top of the paper bag two times so it can stand up on its own. Decorate the bag as desired. Construction paper and doilies were used for the bag shown here.

Paper Plate Valentine Container

You will need:

2 oval 10" x 12⅝" paper plates
Stapler
Items to decorate the paper plates
X-acto knife

Staple the edges of the paper plates so the bottoms of the plates are facing out. With an X-acto knife make a cut large enough for Valentines to fit through. Decorate the paper plates and the container is ready to fill with Valentine cards.

Mystery Valentine Messages

Pinprick Valentine

You will need: *Paper, needle*

Write out a Valentine message by using a needle to poke holes in the shape of alphabet letters in a piece of paper. The words can easily be seen if the message is held up to the light.

Invisible Ink Valentine

You will need: *Pan of water, ball point pen or medium hard lead pencil (not sharp), 2 sheets white typing paper*

Dip sheet of paper into water; then flatten against hard, smooth surface (window pane, mirror, etc.). Top with dry sheet of paper and write secret message on it, pressing pen down hard. Remove dry sheet and throw away. As first sheet dries, message disappears. To make message reappear, dip paper into water again.

Paper Bowl Valentine Hat

You will need:

1 6" paper bowl
Paper punch
Yarn
Colored paper
Sequins
Foil
Doilies
Glitter
Glue

Punch holes around the top of the bowl and turn the bowl upside down. Cut out hearts and cupids and decorate them with sequins, glitter, doilies and foil. Punch holes in the shapes and tie them onto the bowl. In two holes opposite from each other, secure long pieces of yarn to tie around the chin. The hat is ready to wear.

Valentine Love Potion

Heat the pineapple juice, lemon juice, 3 cups cold water and sugar until mixture is clear. Mix cherry gelatin in hot water until dissolved. Add almond extract. Combine the two mixtures; pour into coffee cans or plastic containers and freeze. Half an hour before serving, remove from freezer and let thaw at room temperature in a punch bowl. Pour ginger ale over mixture.

You will need:

1 quart pineapple juice
½ cup lemon juice concentrate
3 cups cold water
2 cups sugar
1 3-oz. package of cherry gelatin dessert
2 cups hot water
½ teaspoon almond extract
1 quart ginger ale
Coffee cans
Saucepans

Irish Recipes

Baked or Barbecued Irish Potatoes

1 *russet potato per person*
Butter
Sour cream
Cheese spread

Scrub the potatoes and wrap them in aluminum foil. Bury them in hot coals or place them in the oven. Bake for an hour or until a fork can easily pierce the potatoes. With a knife, split each potato down the middle and place butter, sour cream, or cheese spread inside. The Irish potatoes are ready to eat.

Mulligan Stew

2 *cups diced carrots*
1 *cup sliced potatoes*
1 *cup fresh or canned string beans*
1 *cup sliced celery*
1 *cup sliced bell pepper*
1 *cup sliced onion*
¼ *cup all-purpose flour*
1 *3-oz. package dry onion soup mix*
3 *cups diced, cooked beef*
3 *cups water*

Combine the flour and soup mix in a large skillet. Add the water to the mixture in the skillet and heat it to a boil, stirring constantly. Add the vegetables and beef; cover and cook over low heat for 1–1½ hours or until the vegetables are tender.

Leprechaun Puppet

1. Use the pieces of vegetables to decorate the bell pepper face of the leprechaun. Hold the vegetable pieces in place with toothpicks. A construction paper hat or necktie may be added.

2. With the knife, cut a hole in the bottom of the bell pepper large enough for the index finger to fit inside.

You will need: *1 bell pepper*
Pieces of carrot, radish, celery, squash, parsley, etc.
Toothpicks
Scissors

Knife
Green scarf, facial tissue or cloth
Green and white construction paper

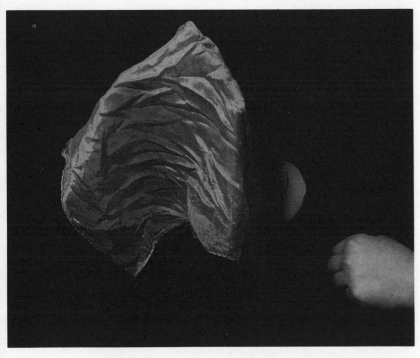

3. Hold up the index finger. Drape the scarf, tissue, or material over the finger, completely covering the hand.

4. Put the index finger and scarf through the hole and the Leprechaun Puppet is ready to play.

69

St. Patrick's Day Hat

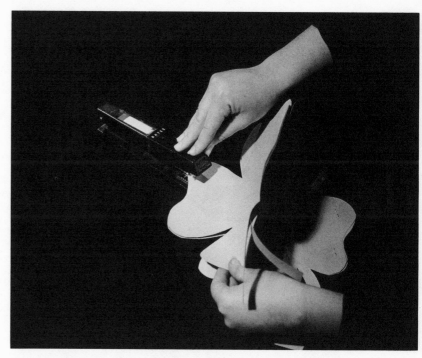

1. Cut out three identical 9″ shamrocks.

2. Place two shamrocks together and staple at one side. Staple one side of the third shamrock to the open side of the upper shamrock. Staple the other side of the third shamrock to the unstapled side of the lower shamrock.

You will need: *3 pieces of green construction paper*
                              Pencil
                              Scissors

3. The St. Patrick's Day Hat is ready to wear. The size of the hat can be adjusted by changing the position of the staples.

Matzo Bag

1. Fold one white and one blue felt square in half to measure 6″ x 9″. Iron the folds.

2. Place the two pieces together with the folds on the bottom, and pin them in place. Whip stitch around the sides of the felt, and the folded bottoms, leaving the top open.

You will need: 2 9″ x 12″ blue felt squares   Pins
1 9″ x 12″ white felt square   Glue
Blue yarn   Scissors
Needle (eye must be large enough   Iron
for yarn to pass through)

3. Cut out two identical triangles from the blue felt and glue one on top of the other on the white side of the bag to resemble a Jewish star.

4. The bag will hold three pieces of matzo (recipe, p. 75). During Passover, Jewish families eat matzos in remembrance of the hardships of the Hebrews' long flight from Egypt, when their bread had to be baked in the hot desert sun.

Jewish Star

You will need: *1 sheet construction paper, glue, scissors, ruler*

1. Cut out two 4″ x 4″ x 4″ triangles. From the center of each triangle cut out a 2″ x 2″ x 2″ triangle. Discard the small triangles. Cut through one side of one triangle near a corner. Place triangle on table, using cut side as base. Hold other triangle by point so top is level; slip right point through cut base of other triangle so right point is under right side of cut triangle.

2. Glue in place. This Jewish star may be made into a necklace with a string through it or can be pinned on a shirt or blouse. **Variation:** Use popsicle sticks or toothpicks to make star. Glue sticks for one triangle and let dry; then weave other sticks in place and glue.

Passover Recipes

Matzo

3½ cups flour
1 cup water

Preheat oven to 475°. Mix flour and water together. Roll dough out on floured board and transfer it to greased cookie sheet. Score large piece of dough into squares with a knife and poke holes in it with a fork. Bake for 10 to 15 minutes or until golden brown.

Haroseth

6 medium apples, grated or chopped very fine
½ cup raisins
½ teaspoon cinnamon
¼ cup grape juice
½ cup chopped nuts

Mix all the ingredients together and serve. This Hebrew food symbolizes the sweetness of freedom to the Jews.

Easter Bonnet

1. Turn the paper bowl upside down on the bottom of the paper plate. Staple or glue them together. A hole for the head may be cut in the paper plate.

2. On each side of the paper plate, punch a hole and tie a piece of ribbon or yarn through it.

You will need:

1 paper plate	Glue
1 paper bowl	Scissors
Assorted colors of tissue paper	Ribbon or yarn
Assorted colors of crepe paper streamers	Stapler
	Paper punch

3. Decorate the hat with streamers, ribbon, yarn, etc.

4. The bonnet is ready to be worn. Tie it under the child's chin.

Bunny Bag Puppet

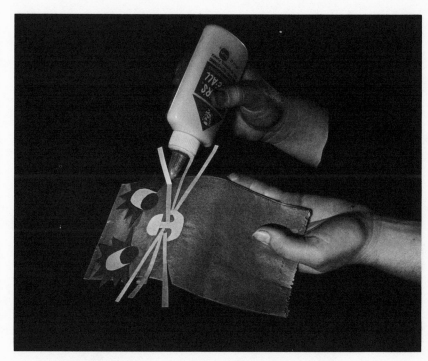

1. Open up the bag and on the bottom cut two holes an inch apart. This will now become the top of the puppet.

2. On the front of the puppet, have the child draw facial features or paste features cut from colored construction paper.

You will need: 1 4″ x 7½″ paper bag
Crayons
Scissors
Cotton
Glue

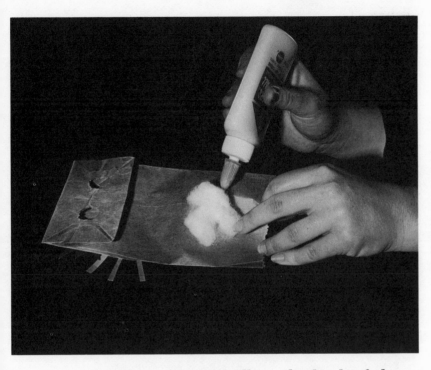

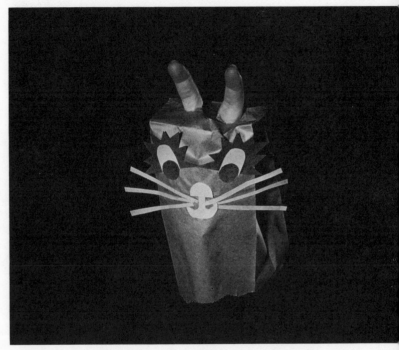

3. Glue a cotton ball on the back of the puppet for the tail.

4. The puppet is ready to use. Place one hand in the bag and stick two fingers out of the holes for the bunny's ears.

Paper Bag Easter Basket

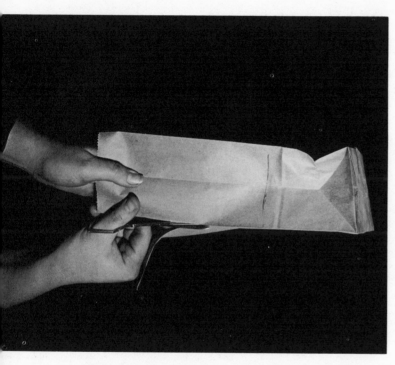

1. With the bag open, cut a 7" slit along one corner toward the bottom of the bag. Repeat on the other three corners of the bag.

2. At the end of each slit, cut the front and back off the bag, leaving two sides, which will become the handles.

You will need: *1 5½″ x 10½″ paper lunch bag*
Scissors
Staples or tape

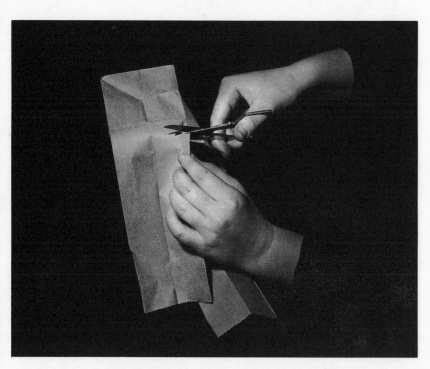

3. Now make a 1″ cut on each side of the handles in line with the top of the basket. Fold the sides of the handles to the middle for added strength.

4. Tape or staple the two handles together. The basket is ready to use. Grass, flowers, Easter eggs, and candy may be carried in it.

81

More Easter Baskets

Strawberry Carton Basket

Plastic Bottle Basket

You will need: *1 strawberry or cherry tomato plastic carton, 1 or 2 pipe cleaners, assorted colors of yarn or ribbon, scissors*

Weave assorted colors of yarn or ribbon through holes of carton. Decorate if desired. For handle, connect the pipe cleaners together securely at one end. Attach loose ends to opposite sides of basket.

You will need: *Bleach bottle or plastic water or milk container, 15″ piece of rope, paper punch, scissors, glue, assorted colors tissue paper and paintbrush* (*optional*)

Cut off top of bottle 5″ from bottom. Punch or cut holes on opposite sides. Tie one end of rope through each hole. Decoupage with watered-down glue and assorted pieces of tissue paper if desired.

Note: All of these baskets may be used for May Day baskets as well as for Easter baskets.

Paper Cup Basket

Paper Bowl Basket

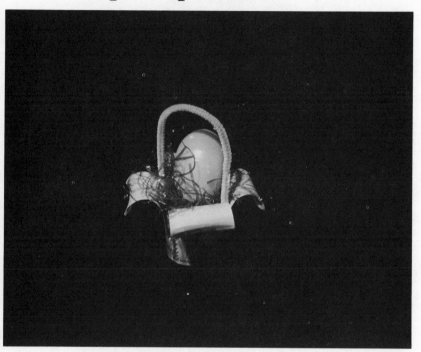

You will need: *7-oz. or 9-oz. waxed paper cup, scissors, pencil, long pipe cleaner, paper punch*

Cut four 2″ slits from top to middle of cup equal distances apart. With pencil, curl each piece of cup. Punch holes on opposite sides of cup. For handle, secure one end of pipe cleaner in each hole.

You will need: *6″ paper bowl, 1½″ x 15″ piece of tagboard, stapler*

Staple the piece of tagboard on opposite sides of bowl. Decorate handle and bowl with stickers, pictures from magazines, wrapping paper, etc.

Ice Cream Carton Basket

Gift Box Basket

You will need: *1 ice cream or milk carton with top removed, scissors, stapler*

On opposite sides of carton, mark two 1½″-wide strips. Those will become the handle. Draw line all the way around carton 3″ from bottom. Cut along each side of 1½″ handles to this 3″ line. Then cut along 3″ line leaving handles in place. Staple handles together over basket. Decorate as desired.

You will need: *Gift box, thick yarn, scissors, paper punch*

Punch three holes 1–2″ apart on one side of box. On opposite side, punch three holes in same positions. Cut three pieces of yarn for handle. Tie one piece of yarn through each hole, on same side of box. Braid yarn to desired length. Secure each end of yarn to hole on opposite side.

84

How to Hard-boil an Egg without Cracking the Shell

You will need:

1 or more eggs
  Bowl
  Saucepan
  Water
  Spoon

Place eggs in bowl of warm water. Fill saucepan with enough water to cover eggs 1″. Heat water to boil. With spoon, transfer eggs from warm water to boiling water. Reduce heat under saucepan to below simmering and cook eggs 20 minutes. Immediately cool eggs in cold water to prevent from further cooking. When eggs are cool they are ready to decorate. Hard-boiled eggs may be kept for many years.

Egg inside shell eventually will dry up into a ball which will rattle when egg is shaken. If shell is broken before contents disintegrate, odor is overwhelming. If egg is to be eaten, keep it in refrigerator until ready to use.

How to Blow Out an Eggshell

1. Use pin to pierce hole in large (round) end of egg. Do this carefully by twisting pin back and forth until hole is made through shell and membrane of egg.

2. On pointed end of egg, make another hole with pin and enlarge it carefully by breaking bits of shell away with point of pin. This hole should not exceed ¼″ in diameter.

You will need: 1 egg at room temperature
1 hat pin, corsage pin, or large needle
1 bowl

3. Push pin inside egg to break and mix up yolk and white well. Put fingers over holes and shake up well. (This will allow contents to come out more easily.)

4. Hold egg over bowl with large end down. Carefully blow through small hole until contents are all out. Rinse shell out with water and store in egg carton to dry. Be sure to remove from the mouth any lipstick, chapstick, or other greasy substances; this will prevent paint from adhering to the shell. When egg is completely dry, paint or decorate it with beads, glitter, etc.

Speedy Easter Egg Dye

You will need:

2 *tablespoons of vinegar*
Few drops of food coloring (any color)
Small dish
Hard-boiled egg
Spoon
Newspaper
Cake rack

Pour vinegar into dish and stir in food coloring one drop at a time to achieve desired color. Roll the egg around in the dish, spooning dye over it. This works in seconds. For darker colors, leave egg in longer. For speckled eggs, leave egg in twenty minutes and continue to spoon dye over it. Mix up several colors of egg dye. For multicolored eggs, put parts of egg into different colors. Dry eggs on cake rack. Put newspaper under cake rack to catch drops of color. Water will wash off this speedy egg dye.

Crayon Resist Eggs

You will need:

1 *hard-boiled egg*
1 *white crayon*
1 *dish of egg dye*
   Paper towel

Draw picture or design on eggshell with white crayon. Dip egg into dye and turn egg until it has reached color desired. Lift out egg, and picture will be white. Place egg on paper towels to dry. **Variation:** Instead of using crayon to draw picture, use rubber cement to squiggle designs on eggshell. Hold egg in hand a few minutes to dry. Place egg into dye until coloring is complete. Dry color thoroughly and then remove rubber cement from dry eggshell with fingers.

Easter Bulletin Board

Have the teacher make a big brown Easter basket from construction paper. Give each child an egg shape to decorate with crayons, felt tip markers, or glue and glitter. Let each child pin his egg in the basket or on the ground next to it.

You will need:

Brown construction paper
Assorted colors of construction paper
Crayons or felt tip markers
Scissors
Glue and glitter (optional)
Straight pins

Lady Bug

You will need:

1 black pipe cleaner
2 plastic eyes
1 2" styrofoam ball
   Red paint
   Black paint
   Black sequins
   Straight pins
   Knife
   Paintbrush
   Glue

Cut styrofoam ball in half. On one half, paint shape of lady bug in black and red. Let it dry. Attach sequins with straight pins for spots on wings. Glue on eyes and add pipe cleaners for antennae. The lady bug is ready to use as a bulletin board idea or centerpiece.

May Day Baskets

Paper Plate Basket I

Paper Plate Basket II

You will need: *9" paper plate, 2" x 10" piece of tagboard, stapler*

Fold paper plate in half. Fold piece of tagboard in half for handle. Staple ends of handle to top of plate on each side. Decorate basket with stickers, glitter, magazine pictures or marking pens. Put flowers inside the basket to give a friend.

You will need: *2 9" paper plates*
Scissors
Stapler

Staple edges of two plates together all the way around. Cut out a half circle from top halves of each plate. Decorate front of basket and it is ready to fill with May Day flowers.

92

Note: These baskets may also be used for Easter baskets.

Folded Basket

Butterfly Basket

You will need: *12" x 12" square of construction paper, 1½" x 10" piece of construction paper, scissors, stapler or glue, pencil, ruler*

Divide 12" square into 9 equal squares; number across left to right, 1-9. Cut bottom line of square 1; right side line of 7; top line of 9; left side line of 3. Fold along every line that was drawn and form into paper basket. Staple or glue sides together and staple handle on. Decorate basket and fill with flowers.

You will need: *1½" x 10" piece of construction paper, 12" x 18" piece of construction paper, scissors, stapler*

Fold 12" x 18" piece of paper in half to measure 12" x 9". Draw a butterfly with bottom of body on fold; cut out except for fold. Staple shut outside edge of each wing and top of butterfly's head. On inside of each wing, staple one end of handle. Decorate and fill with flowers.

93

Tissue Paper Flowers I

1. Fan-fold the squares of tissue paper.

2. Wrap the floral wire tightly around the center of the folded tissue paper.

You will need: 6   *4" x 4" squares of tissue paper*
                               Floral wire
                               Floral tape
                               Scissors

3. Open the folds and separate the sheets of tissue paper from the middle of the flower.

4. Cover the wire with floral tape. Green tissue paper leaves may be added when the stem is being taped. The Tissue Paper Flower is ready to be put in a May Day basket.

Tissue Paper Flowers II

1. Fold the paper in half lengthwise.

2. Fold one of the ends into a triangle.

You will need: *1 4" x 6" piece of tissue paper*
Floral wire
Floral tape
Scissors

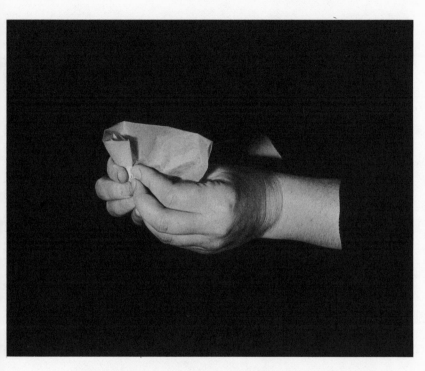

3. Beginning with the folded end, gather the paper into a circle at the open edge to form a flower bud.

4. Wire the gathered edge together and cover with floral tape, adding tissue paper leaves if desired. The flower bud is ready to be used in a May Day basket.

May Pole

1. Lay pole on ground. Tape or thumb-tack tissue paper flowers to top of pole if desired. Tape one end of all the streamers onto sides of top of pole. Extend tops of streamers above pole. Cut out twelve 3-yard pieces of ribbon and tape over streamers. If May Pole is to be used outdoors, bury bottom of pole in hole in ground. If it is to be used inside, mount in a Christmas tree stand.

2. Various steps can be used in wrapping the May Pole. *Single Wrap:* Number children from 1 to 4, going to right. All to go right for 32 counts, to their original position. *Double Wrap:* Odd numbers go to left 32 counts, holding ribbons up high. Evens go to right and under odds' ribbons. Unwrap for 32 counts back to position.

You will need:

1	7–10′ pole
36	yards of ribbon
	Thumbtacks
	Tape

Tissue paper flowers, crepe paper, or ribbon streamers

Christmas tree stand (for indoor use)

Spider Web

Odds take one step in and go down on one knee, holding ribbons high. Evens go to right and under odds, taking 16 counts to move to four people and 16 counts to return to original position.

Cross

Number ones walk to pole in 8 counts with left shoulder next to pole, facing right. Number twos go in and line up shoulder to shoulder with number ones (8 counts); then threes (8 counts) and fours (8 counts). All move together, taking half steps and looking toward pole for 16 counts. Return to pole in 16 counts. Return to normal position, allowing 8 counts each for fours, threes, twos, and ones.

May Day Bulletin Board

Cut out flower shapes from construction paper. Have each child decorate his flower. With the straight pins and pieces of green yarn make grass on the base of the bulletin board. Mount the flowers up on the board on a green yarn stem.

You will need:

Thick green yarn
Straight pins
Assorted spring colors of construction paper
Crayons or markers, tissue paper decoupage, eggshell collage, rickracks, laces, doilies, stickers, etc.

Halloween Make-up

Note: For more ideas on masks and costumes refer to *The Great Pretenders* and *More Great Pretenders* by Joy Wilt and Cathy Berry (Waco, Tx.: Creative Resources, 1978).

You will need:

Cornstarch
Shortening
Food coloring
Small bar cocoa butter
3″ square of aluminum foil
Fat pencil or felt-tip pen
Saucepan and potholder
Spoon
Small drinking glass
Small funnel

For **face make-up** blend 1 part shortening to 2 parts cornstarch and a few drops of desired color of food coloring. Mix until creamy, and it is ready to put on face or body. Dusting with talcum powder will help set make-up. For **lipstick** wrap aluminum foil around blunt end of pencil. Twist one end closed and slip off pencil. Put 1 teaspoon of cocoa butter in saucepan and melt over low heat. Remove from stove and stir in ¼ teaspoon cornstarch until smooth. Add food coloring until desired color is achieved. Prop piece of aluminum foil inside a glass and pour lipstick into it through funnel. Place lipstick in refrigerator for 10 minutes to set. Open one end of lipstick, round edges with fingers, and it is ready to use. Keep lipstick in cool place because cocoa butter melts at body temperature.

101

Ice Cream Cone Witch

You will need:

1 *cup ice cream*
1 *large round cookie*
1 *sugar ice cream cone*
1 *cupcake paper*
  Frosting
  Decorations, candies, raisins, nuts, etc.
  Ice cream scoop

Place one scoop of ice cream into cupcake paper. Place cookie on top and press into ice cream to secure in place. Frost ice cream cone onto cookie to make witch's hat. Decorate face with frosting, candies, raisins, nuts, etc. Place in freezer until ready to eat.

Pumpkin and Vegetable Carving

You will need:

Pumpkin
Turnips
Parsnips
Squashes
Gourds
Carrots
Apples
Radishes
Potatoes
Felt tip pen
Knife
Spoon

The traditional way to carve a pumpkin is to cut a small circle around the stem and remove that piece. Clean the inside, removing the strings and seeds. Draw a face on the pumpkin with a felt tip pen and cut it out with a knife no sooner than two days before Halloween so it will last. Instead of carving, pumpkins may be decorated with vegetable pieces for the face. Shadow carvings on the rind of the pumpkin can also be used. Other large vegetables make novel Halloween cut-ups as well by using the same methods.

HALLOWEEN
Paper Bag Jack-o'-lantern

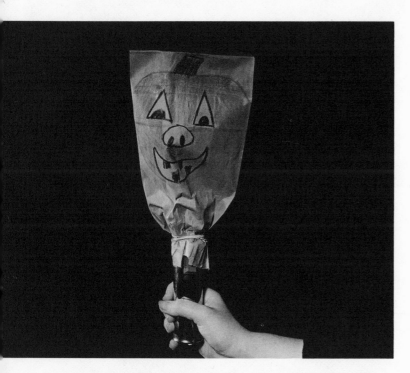

1 *paper lunch bag*
1 *flashlight with batteries*
   Crayons
   Rubber band

Draw a jack-o'-lantern on each side of the paper bag. Place the bag over the light of the flashlight and secure with a rubber band. Turn the flashlight on and the paper bag jack-o'-lantern is ready to guide a trick-or-treater on Halloween night. Parts of the face may be cut out to allow the jack-o'-lantern to give off more light.

Paper Sack Treat Bag

You will need:

1 large paper sack
1 2" x 18" piece of tagboard
  Scissors
  Colored paper
  Marking pens
  Stickers
  Glue

Fold down the top of the bag two times. Staple tagboard onto the bag for a handle. Decorate the bag with stickers, colored paper, cutouts, or drawings. The bag is ready to gather Halloween treats.

Pillowcase Treat Bag

You will need:

1 pillowcase
   Waterproof marking pens

Draw Halloween pictures on the pillow-case, and the bag is ready to use for trick or treat.

Oatmeal Box Treat Bag

You will need:

1 oatmeal box
1 12″ piece of rope
   Colored paper
   Glue
   Scissors
   Paper punch
   Marking pens
   Stickers

Cover the box with colored paper. Decorate the box with stickers, paper cutouts, or marking pens. Punch two holes on opposite sides and tie the ends of the rope in the holes for the handle.

Witches' Brews

Bubbling Cauldron
(Apple Cider Punch)

1   gallon apple cider
3   large cans pineapple juice (16 cups)
6   cups apricot nectar
4   cups orange juice
4   teaspoons whole cloves
½   box cinnamon sticks, broken

Combine all the ingredients and simmer until warm. This can be served warm from a kettle or a punch bowl. The spices float on top.

Enchanted Elixir
(Mulled Cider)

1   cup apple cider
1   teaspoon honey or sugar
    Slice of lemon
    Cinnamon sticks
    Saucepan
    Knife
    Strainer

Place the apple cider, honey, lemon slice, and cinnamon stick in the saucepan. Heat to a boil. Place a small strainer over a cup and pour the cider into the cup. Stir with cinnamon stick until cool enough to drink.

Window Murals

You will need:

1 cup Bon Ami
1 cup Alabastrine (glass paint or whitening, available at most paint stores)
1 cup dry tempera paint
Water

Mix the ingredients together, using enough water to make a paint with a pastel-like consistency. Paint the mixture on a window with a brush. This can easily be washed off with water. Make as many colors as necessary to paint the Halloween mural on the windows.

Skeleton Decoration

1. Place the 4″ x 18″ piece of paper as shown. Cut a cross in center of paper, 3½″ vertically and 2″ horizontally. From the 10″ x 10″ piece of paper, cut out any body shape. At one end of 8″ x 10″ piece of paper, cut a T shape 1″ x 5″ across and 1″ x 2″ up and down. Continue the 1″ x 2″ section into a head shape. Draw face with marking pens.

2. Attach the T section through the slits on the 4″ x 18″ paper and glue it in place. Glue the body to this piece also.

You will need: 1 4″ x 18″ piece of white paper   Marking pen
1 10″ x 10″ piece of white paper   Glue
1 8″ x 10″ piece of white paper   Scissors
6 6″ circles of white paper

3. Cut spirals out of the six circles. Attach two spirals together for each leg.

4. Attach the legs and arms to the skeleton and he is ready to hang up.

111

Witch Door Decoration

1. Fold the 11″ x 19″ piece of yellow construction paper every 4¾″.

2. Cut or draw a face on the folded yellow piece of paper. The third fold is the middle of the face.

You will need: 1 18″ x 24″ piece of tagboard
3 12″ x 18″ pieces black construction
    paper
1 11″ x 19″ piece of yellow construction
    paper

Yarn
Glue
Scissors
Marking pen
Stapler

3. From the black paper, cut an 18″ x 4″ x 18″ x 12″ trapezoid for the hat. Make 1″ folds along each 18″ side. For brim of hat, cut an 18″-diameter half-circle with a 4″ x 4″ tab in the middle of the straight edge. Fold brim in half.

4. Attach face by gluing the two side folds to the large piece of tagboard. Attach tab of hat brim to tagboard and rest brim on witch's face. Glue hat to tagboard so it rests on brim. Add the words "Happy Halloween" and the door decoration is ready to hang.

Pilgrim Collar

You will need: *1 12" x 18" piece of white paper*
Scissors

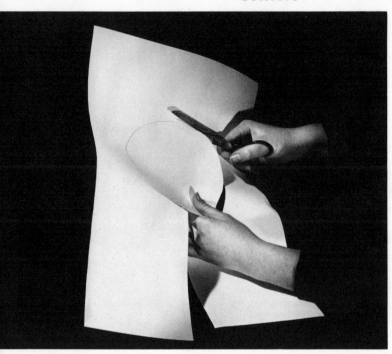

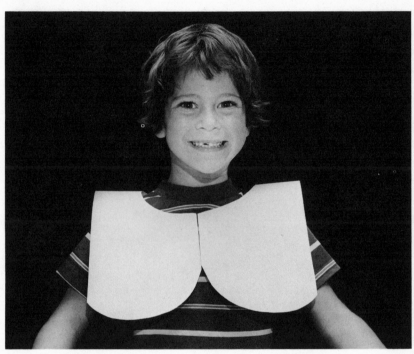

1. From the middle of the 12" side of the paper, cut in 7" toward the center of the paper. From the end of that slit, cut out a circle 6" in diameter. Round off the corners of the vest front to resemble photo 2.

2. To wear, place the slit in front and the circle around the neck.

Girl's Pilgrim Hat

You will need: *1 #12 paper bag*
Scissors

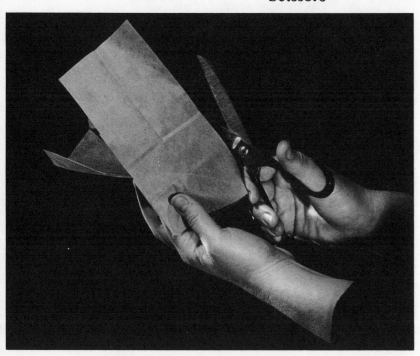

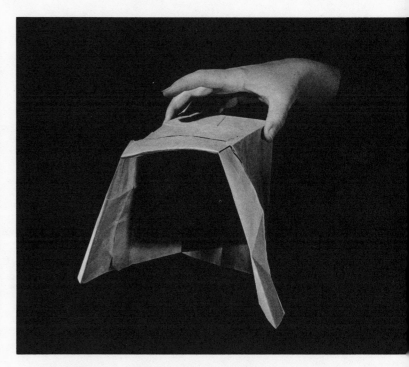

1. Measure 8″ down from the top of the bag and cut the bag off all around at that point, saving the bottom portion. Cut out one of the smaller sides of the bag.

2. Fold back the three edges that are left about 1″, and the hat is ready to wear.

115

Boy's Pilgrim Hat

1. From the inside of the 10½" circle, cut out a 6½" circle. Save this circle. Use the quarter-circle to make a cone shape, gluing or stapling it in place.

2. Cut off the top of the cone and make slits around the top and bottom. Fold the bottom ends out and glue them around the inner edge of the 10½" circle. Fold the top ends in and glue them to the 6½" circle, cutting this down to fit.

116

You will need: *1 10½" circle of gray paper*   *Glue*
                      1 gray paper quarter-circle, 16" radius   *Scissors*
                      1 2" x 12" piece of black paper   *Stapler*
                      1 4" x 4" piece of yellow paper

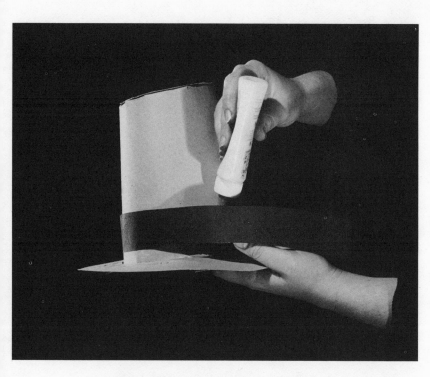

3. Glue the black piece of paper around the base of the hat.

4. Cut out a 3" x 3" square from the center of the yellow square to make a buckle. Glue this on top of the black strip in the center front, and the hat is ready to wear for the Thanksgiving celebration.

Indian Vest

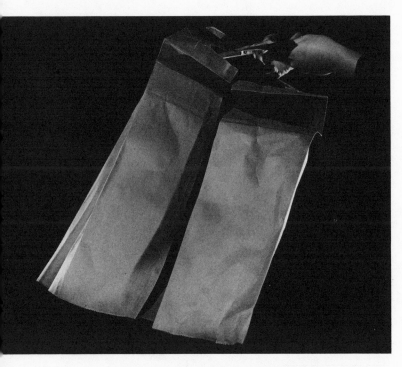

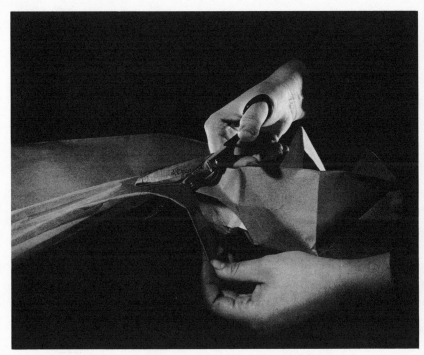

1. On the front center of the bag cut down to the bottom. Make a 3″ cut on the bottom, and from it make a 7″ circular cut for the neck.

2. On each side of the bag, about 4″ from the neck opening, cut a circle large enough for the arm to go through.

You will need: 1 *large grocery bag*
Scissors

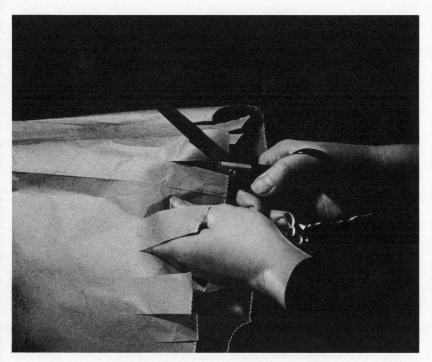

3. Make 2″ vertical cuts all the way around the open end of the bag.

4. The Indian vest is ready to wear.

Roll the Ball Indian Game

You will need:

1 *coffee can*
1 *bag of beans*
1 *rock for every player*
1 *6" square of cardboard*
1 *ball*

Place the cardboard on top of the coffee can. Place six beans on top of the cardboard. From a distance of 10–20 feet, players take turns rolling the ball to knock down the coffee can. Each marks the spot with a rock where their ball lands. When the target is knocked over, each player keeps the beans nearest where his ball landed. The winner is the one with the most beans.

120

Kick the Stick Indian Relay

You will need:

1 1' crooked stick for each team
1 marked goal

Have each team line up behind their stick, the same distance from the goal (about 20 feet). The first player on each team kicks the stick along the ground, to the goal and back. Each player in turn kicks the stick to the goal and back. The team that finishes first wins.

121

Harvest Recipes

Corn Pudding

3 beaten eggs
2 cups drained, cooked or canned whole
    kernel corn
2 cups scalded milk
⅓ cup finely chopped onion
1 tablespoon melted butter
1 teaspoon sugar
1 teaspoon salt

Preheat oven to 350°. Combine all ingredients and pour into a greased 1½-quart casserole dish. Add 1″ of hot water to a shallow pan large enough to hold the casserole dish. Set the casserole dish in it and place in oven. Bake 40–45 minutes or until a knife inserted in center comes out clean. Let stand at room temperature for 10 minutes before serving.

Cranberry Sauce

2 cups sugar
2 cups water
4 cups fresh cranberries

Combine sugar and water in a saucepan and stir until sugar dissolves. Heat to boiling and boil for 5 minutes. Add cranberries and cook until skins pop (about 5 minutes). Remove from heat and serve warm or chilled.

Thank You Bulletin Board

Have the children cut pictures from a magazine of things they are thankful for. Make a giant collage of these on the bulletin board.

You will need:

Magazines
Pins
Scissors

Dreidel

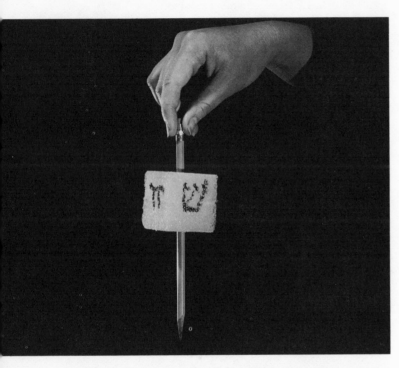

1 *2" x 2" x 2" cube of styrofoam*
   Pencil with sharp point
   Letters
   Marking pen

Insert the pencil through the middle of the styrofoam cube. A dreidel is a top Jewish children play a game with at Hanukkah. On each side of the dreidel put the Hebrew letters:

נ nun ג gimel ה he ש shin

These words mean "A great miracle happened there." Spin the dreidel like a top to see who can spin theirs the longest or to see which letter lands on top the most.

124

Potato Latkes

Mix the potatoes, egg, onion, flour and salt together in a bowl. In the frying pan melt the margarine. Drop the mixture by large rounded tablespoons into the pan. Fry on both sides and serve hot with sour cream or applesauce.

You will need:

Bowl
Frying pan
Spoon

Recipe:
   4 *grated potatoes (squeeze out moisture with paper towel)*
   1 *egg*
   1 *small onion, grated (optional)*
   1 *tablespoon flour*
      Dash of salt
      Margarine

Hanukkah Candles

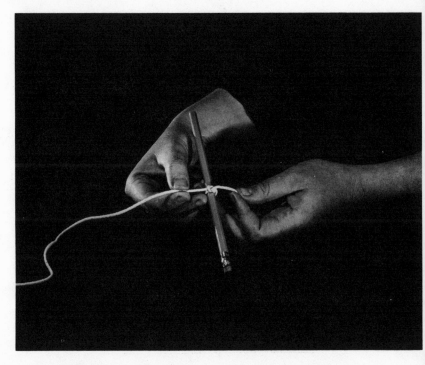

1. Break paraffin into pieces and melt it slowly in a double boiler. Don't boil or overheat paraffin; it could ignite. If colored candles are desired, add some wax crayons, beeswax, and hardener for better burning. Tie wick on middle of dowel, making it 2″ shorter than depth of coffee can.

You will need: *1 dowel for every candle*   *Newspaper*
                              Wicks   *Coffee can*
                              Paraffin   *2 poles or broomsticks*
                              Old double boiler   *2 chairs*
                              Large pot

2. Pour hot water into tub or large pot. Then pour boiling water into coffee can up to 3″ from top. Pour wax on top of boiling water. Keep level of wax about 3″, adding more as needed. Keep wax warm, but not so hot that it melts the paraffin off the wick or so cool that it hardens in the pot. Dip wick into wax and lift it up. Allow to cool for a minute and shape with fingers. Continue dipping until shape is set and firm. Place broomsticks over two chairs; cover floor with paper and place dowel over sticks to allow candle to dry.

Yule Log

You will need: *Newspaper*
Masking tape

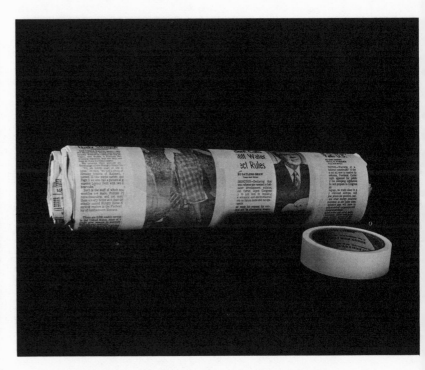

1. Fold 10 individual sheets of newspaper in half. Overlap the folded sheets and roll into a loose cylinder approximately 4″ in diameter.

2. Tape the cylinder shut and place under the wood to get the fire started.

Drapery Ring Wreath

You will need: *1 wooden drapery ring, green yarn, sequins or felt pieces, scissors*

1. With the yarn tie a knot on the drapery ring. Tie half hitches all the way around the ring. (To tie a half hitch, make a loop on front side of ring, making sure left side of loop crosses over right side. Take free end of string behind drapery ring, then forward through loop, and pull tight.)

2. Decorate the wreath with the sequins or felt pieces and it is ready to hang on the tree.

Christmas Tree Chains

Poptop Chain

You will need: *100 or more pop-tops from soft drink cans*

Take end of poptop that was attached to can and put it through circle of another poptop. Close end tight. Continue building on chain until it is desired length.

Popcorn Chain

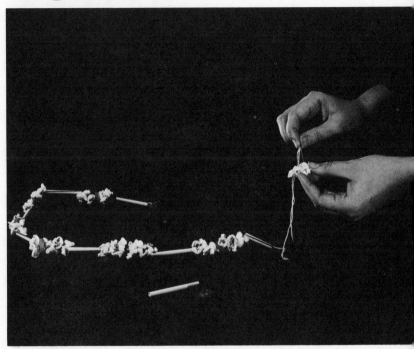

You will need: *Popcorn, Lifesavers, straws (cut into fourths), string, needle*

Thread string through needle. Tie a Lifesaver on end of string. Thread several pieces of popcorn on string, then a Lifesaver, more pieces of popcorn, piece of straw, more popcorn, Lifesaver, popcorn, straw, etc. Repeat until the chain is desired length.

Paper Chain

Bell Chain

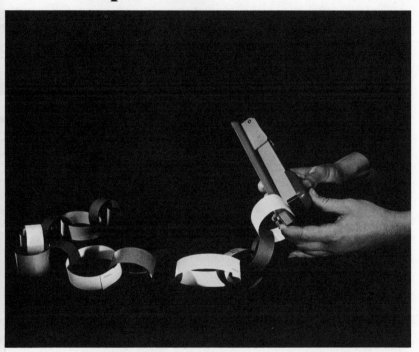

You will need: *Several sheets of red, green, and white construction paper; glue or stapler; scissors*

Cut strips of paper 1″ x 9″. Staple opposite ends of one strip to form a circle. Put another strip through the first circle. Again staple opposite ends, forming an interlocking chain. Continue until chain is desired length.

You will need: *Egg cartons, needle, yarn, glitter, glue, scissors*

Cut out the individual egg cups from the egg carton. Decorate with glue and glitter. Thread yarn through needle and string egg carton bells onto yarn. Repeat until desired length is reached. A real bell may be hung from each egg cup.

More Christmas Tree Chains

Styrofoam Chains

Braided Chain

You will need: *Pieces of styrofoam packing, needle, thread*

Thread the needle and string pieces of styrofoam packing on the thread until the desired length of chain is reached.

You will need: *Red, green, or white rug yarn or other thick yarn*

Knot three pieces of yarn of the same or varied colors together and braid. When desired length is reached, knot or wrap ends to keep from unwinding.

Star Chain

Tissue Paper Chain

You will need: *Several sheets white construction paper, red yarn, needle*

Cut out many stars from the white construction paper. Thread needle with a long piece of red yarn, and knot end. With needle and yarn, lace stars on yarn, spacing as desired. Continue until chain is long enough to wrap around the tree.

You will need: *Tissue paper, yarn, scissors*

Cut 3″ x 6″ pieces of tissue paper. Fold in half to measure 1½″ x 6″. Place fold on top. Fold top right corner toward bottom to form a triangle. At bottom right corner of triangle, roll bottom edge to form flower bud. Tie buds onto large piece of yarn to form chain of desired length.

Cone Cup Christmas Decoration

You will need: *Cone cup, wooden bead or styrofoam ball, pipe cleaner, yarn, cotton, glue, materials and trims, sequins*

1. Cut a 3″ piece of pipe cleaner, bending one end to form a right angle. Poke the other end through the tip of the cone and on through the bead or styrofoam ball. Secure this in place.

2. Decorate the cone and face with sequins, felt, yarn, etc. These figures can become Mrs. Claus, angels, choir singers, Wise Men, etc.

Walnut Shell Santa

You will need: *Clear nail polish, walnuts, cotton, red felt, glue, scissors*

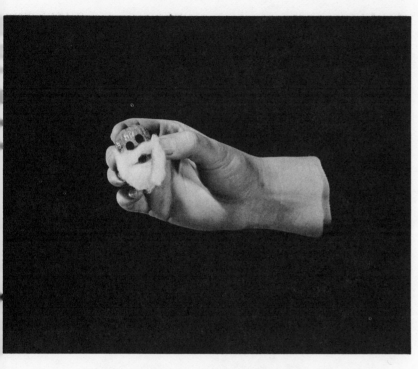

1. Coat the walnut shell with nail polish and let dry. Decorate the face with felt and cotton.

2. Cut a quarter-circle of red felt with a 4″ radius for Santa's hat. Glue the edges together in a cone shape. After the glue is dry, fit the hat on Santa's head, bending down the top and gluing it on the side of Santa's head. To complete the hat, add a white band and ball of cotton.

135

Santa Claus Candy Holder

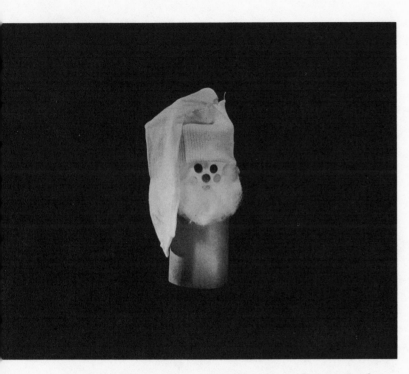

You will need:

1 empty toilet paper tube
  Red, white, and black construction
    paper
  White baby sock
  Cotton
  Glue
  Marking pens

Cut out a circle ¼″ larger than the end of the toilet paper tube. Make ¼″ cuts all the way around the circle and glue this over one end of the tube. Cover tube with a piece of red paper. Draw a Santa Claus face; cut it out and place on one end of tube. Glue on cotton beard. Fill tube with candy and place a baby sock over top for Santa's hat.

Ice Cream Cone Christmas Tree

You will need:

Frosting:
   1 *cup powdered sugar*
   ⅛ *teaspoon salt*
   ⅛ *cup of milk*
   ½ *teaspoon vanilla*
   ⅓ *stick of margarine*
   4 *drops of green food coloring*
Cookie decorations
Popcorn
Ice cream cones

Mix all the frosting ingredients together and beat with an electric mixer until smooth. Place the ice cream cones upside down and have the children frost the cones. Decorate the Christmas trees with the popcorn and cookie decorations.

Stained Glass Window Cookies

You will need:

Mixer
Large bowl
Cookie sheets
Aluminum foil
Sifter

Cookie ingredients:
   3   tablespoons softened butter
   ½   cup light brown sugar
   1   egg
   2   tablespoons water
   ¼   cup molasses
   2   cups flour
   1   teaspoon salt
   ½   teaspoon cinnamon
   ½   teaspoon ginger
   ¼   teaspoon nutmeg
       Assorted colorful hard candies

Cream the butter and sugar together in a large bowl. Add eggs and beat well. Add molasses and water and mix thoroughly. Sift flour, salt, cinnamon, ginger, and nutmeg together, and gradually add to creamed mixture. Mix into dough; then refrigerate for one hour. While dough is chilling, crush candies according to color, keeping separate. Cover a cookie sheet with a piece of aluminum foil and with a toothpick, draw designs (stars, bells, trees, angels) lightly on the foil. Within each design, make several compartments. Work with a small amount of dough to make long thin strips of dough about the width of a pencil. Outline the design with strips of dough. Place crushed candies in each compartment so they reach the top of the dough outline. Preheat the oven to 375° and bake 4–7 minutes or until the candies melt. Place in the refrigerator until completely cooled; then peel off the foil. These cookies can be hung from the Christmas tree or eaten.

138

Christmas Cheer

Orange Wassail

1 cup sugar
1 cup water
1 box of cloves
2 2″ pieces of cinnamon stick
3 quarts orange juice
1 quart cranberry juice cocktail
3 oranges

Make three baked oranges for floating in the punch by sticking whole cloves in the three oranges. Place in a baking dish and bake in 325° oven for 3 hours. Combine sugar, water, cinnamon, and 12 cloves in a saucepan and simmer for 10 minutes. Remove cloves and cinnamon from saucepan. Add orange juice and cranberry juice cocktail and heat. Pour into a heat-proof punch bowl and float the baked oranges on top.

Holly and Ivy Delight

4 quarts lemon-lime soda
2 quarts lime sherbet
1 16-oz. package frozen strawberries, partially thawed
Mint leaves
Large piece of ice

Place ice in 3-gal. punch bowl. Add soda and sherbet. Float strawberries and mint leaves on top.

Christmas Bulletin Board

Cut a Christmas tree out of butcher paper. Fingerpaint the Christmas tree. Using the materials above, have the children make Christmas ornaments. When the tree is dry, place it on the bulletin board and let the children pin their decorations on the tree.

You will need:

Butcher paper
Yarn
Green paint
Pipe cleaners
Foil
Paper
Pens
Felt
Scissors
Pins
Material scraps
Glitter and sequins
Popcorn
Bulletin board

Month by Month Happenings

Paper Bag Party Hat

You will need: 1 *#12 paper bag*
                           Scissors

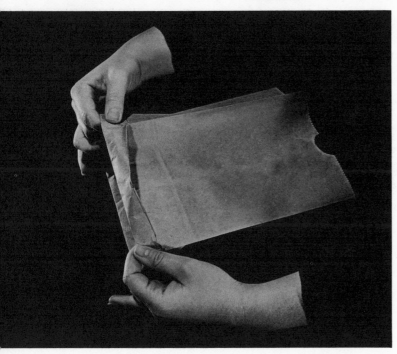

1. Cut the bottom from the bag. Fold the bottom edges up 1″.

2. Fringe the opposite end of bag by making 2″ cuts all the way around the bag. The hat is ready to wear. Place the folded edge on the head. The hat can be worn sticking straight up or twisted in the middle. This hat can be decorated with crayons, stickers, paint, felt, etc.

Screechy Noisemakers

Straw Screamer

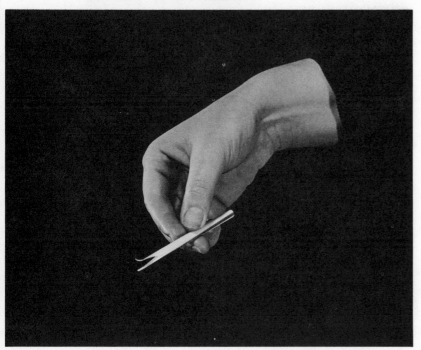

You will need: *1 8" plastic straw*
Scissors

Cut the straw in half. Using one of the halves, flatten about 1" of one end. Cut the flattened end to a point. Place this on the top of the tongue and blow through it to produce a screaming sound.

Balloon Screecher

You will need: *1 balloon*

Blow up a balloon. Hold the opening with the fingers and pull apart. The escaping air will cause the rubber to vibrate and create a screeching sound.

143

Paper Popper

1. Label the corners as shown above: top left corner, A; top right corner, B; bottom left corner, C; and bottom right corner, D.

2. Fold the paper so the following letters meet: fold A to C and B to D; fold A to D and B to C.

You will need: *1 8" x 8" square of typing paper*
Pencil

3. Fold the paper back to the first fold. Push the right top corner down and inward along the previous folds. Do the same with the top left corner.

4. Place the index finger between the two pieces of the right fold, grasping the sides firmly with the other fingers. Give the popper a quick downward snap to open with a pop.

145

Holiday Shakers

Toilet Roll Shaker

You will need: *Toilet paper roll, paper, scissors, rice*

Cut two circles ¼″ larger than end of toilet paper roll. Make ¼″ cuts all the way around the circles. Glue one circle around one end of toilet paper roll. Fill toilet paper roll with one tablespoon of rice; then glue on other circle. Shaker can be decorated with paper, stickers, glitter, etc.

Juice Can Shaker

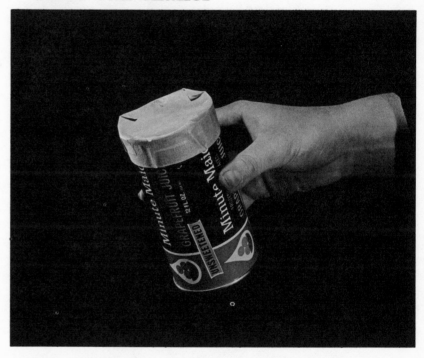

You will need: *Orange juice can with a peel-off lid, tape, dried corn kernels*

Rinse out can and lid thoroughly and dry. Fill with one tablespoon of corn kernels. Tape lid shut and shaker is ready to use. Cover shaker with paper and decorate, if desired.

146

Liquid Sparklers

Grape Sparkler Soda

2 cups grape juice
2 cups ginger ale
8 ice cubes
8 strawberries or raspberries

Mix the grape juice and ginger ale in a pitcher and stir. In each glass, place two ice cubes and two berries. Pour the grape sparkler soda into each glass and enjoy. Serves four.

Pink Panther Punch

4 6-oz. cans raspberry-lemon punch concentrate, partially thawed
1½ quarts ginger ale, chilled
1 lime (or lemon), thinly sliced

Combine partially thawed punch concentrate and ginger ale in large punch bowl. Add ice and float slices of lime or lemon on top.

Lincoln's Log Cabin

You will need:

16 2" or 3" Tootsie Rolls
    Toothpicks
    Cardboard
    Frosting
    Graham cracker

Use the toothpicks and Tootsie Rolls to build a log cabin. Frosting may be used between layers of Tootsie Rolls. Spread frosting on cardboard, and place log cabin on it. Apply frosting to edges of graham cracker to form roof of log cabin.

Lincoln's Slate

You will need:

1 piece of Masonite, approximately
  12" x 18"
1 can chalk board spray paint or black
  flat paint
  Masking tape
  Chalk

Follow the directions on the back of the paint can when spraying. Take a piece of Masonite and spray on chalk board paint, using newspapers to protect from over-spray. After two or three coats are applied and dried, cover the edges with masking tape and the slate is ready to use.

George Washington Tricornered Hat

You will need: *Brown construction paper, stapler, scissors*

1. Cut three 4" x 8" x 10" trapezoids shaped as shown above. Place two trapezoids together and staple one end. Staple the ends of the third trapezoid to the free ends of the first two trapezoids.

2. Spread the sections apart to fit around the head and the hat is ready to wear.

Cherry Cobbler

You will need:

10" x 6" x 1½" baking dish
Saucepan
Bowl
Spoon

Filling:
    1 No. 2 can of pitted tart cherries
    ½ cup sugar
    1 tablespoon quick cooking tapioca
    2 tablespoons butter

Topper:
    1 cup all-purpose flour
    1 tablespoon sugar
  1½ teaspoons baking powder
    ¼ teaspoon salt
    ¼ cup butter
    1 egg
    ¼ cup milk

Combine undrained cherries, sugar and tapioca in a saucepan. Cook and stir mixture until it is thick and clear. Stir in butter. Pour into baking dish and cover with biscuit topper. To make topper, sift together flour, sugar, 1½ teaspoons baking powder and salt. Cut in ¼ cup butter until it resembles coarse crumbs. Mix milk and slightly beaten egg and add all at once to dry ingredients. Stir until moistened. Drop by spoonfuls on top of hot fruit. Bake cobbler at 400° about 20 minutes.

Pinwheel

1. From each corner of the square cut a diagonal slit to 1″ from the middle. When the cuts have been made, you should have 4 equal triangles, joined at their tops.

2. Take the left corner of each triangle and fold it to the middle of the square.

You will need: 1 6″ x 6″ piece of construction paper
1 plastic straw
1 straight pin

1 ½″ x ½″ piece plastic
cut from a drinking
cup

3. Poke a straight pin through the four
corners, through the middle of the
square, through ½″ x ½″ square of
plastic and through the straw.

4. The pinwheel is ready to use in the
wind, in front of an electric fan, or
held in the hand and run with to create a breeze.

Anemometer

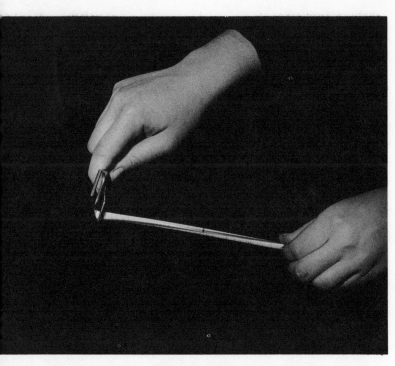

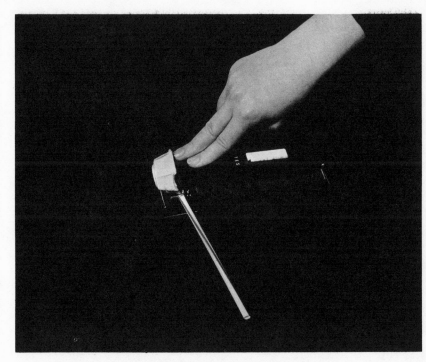

1. Find the middle of each straw and mark it. Flatten about ¾″ of the ends of each straw.

2. Cut four cups from the egg carton. Keep them exactly the same size. Color one cup. Staple one cup to each end of the two straws. The open ends of each cup must face the same direction.

You will need: *2 8″ paper or plastic*   *2 straight pins*
                                     straws   *1 pencil with an eraser*
                                Styrofoam egg carton   *Black marking pen*

3. Attach the two straws to the top of the pencil eraser by sticking the straight pin vertically through the midpoint of the straws.

4. To hold the straws at right angles push the second pin diagonally through straws near the center. The anemometer is ready to use in a gentle breeze. To clock the speed of the wind, count the number of turns the colored cup makes in 30 seconds. Divide by 5 to give the approximate wind speed.

155

Wind Fish

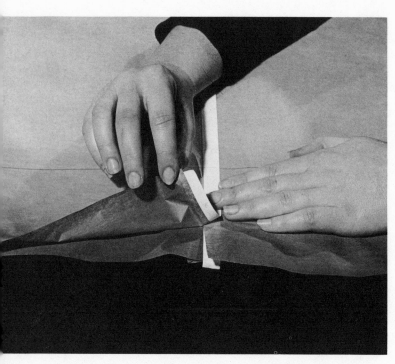

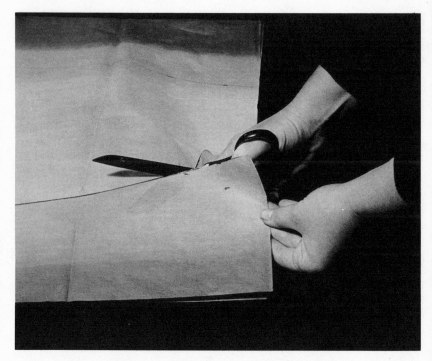

1. Join 3 or 4 sheets of green tissue paper with adhesive tape to form a 5′ length of tissue paper. Two of these will be needed.

2. Place the two sheets of tissue paper together and cut out a shape tapering from 18″ wide on one end to 9″ wide on the other. (See photo for step 8.)

You will need: 8   sheets of green tissue paper   String
                   1   6' stick   Pliers
                   1   3' piece of galvanized wire   Adhesive tape
                       Assorted colors of tissue   Scissors
                           paper

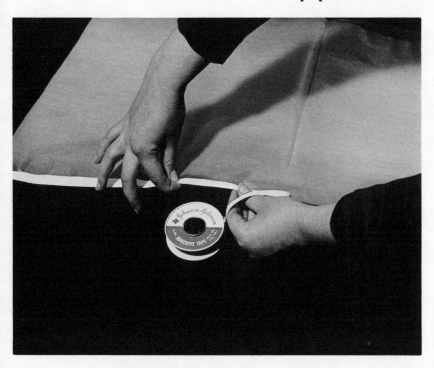

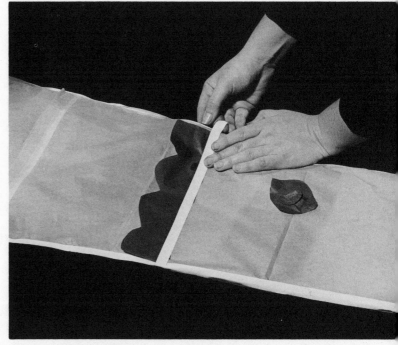

3. Tape the long sides together, leaving both ends open.

4. With other colors of tissue paper, cut out and tape scales, eyes, other decorations on the fish. On the narrow end cut zigzag jaws and tape several red streamers coming out of the mouth.

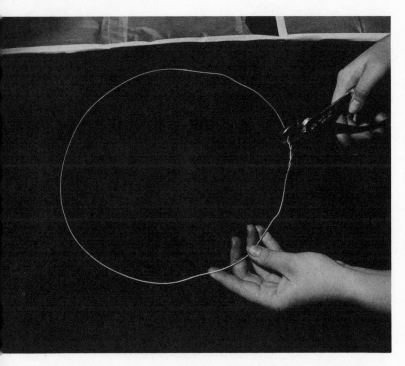

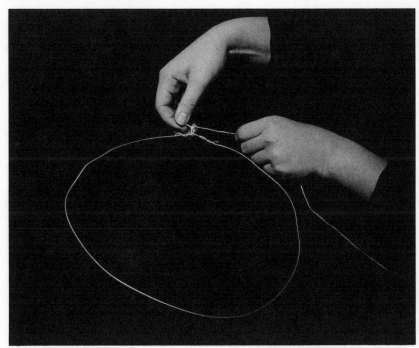

5. With the pliers, bend the galvanized wire into a circle and twist the ends together.

6. Tie four pieces of string to the wire and knot the 4 loose ends together.

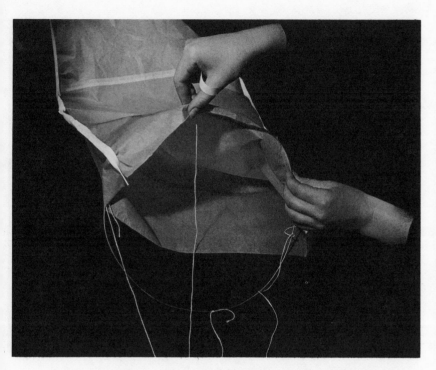

7. Place the wire circle inside the larger open end of the fish and tape it to the ends of the paper with the adhesive tape.

8. Join the four knotted strings to a 12″ piece of string and tie this string to a stick. There should be 5″ of string between the stick and the point at which the single string is tied to the four knotted strings. The wind will fill the fish's body and make it twist in the air.

Kite

1. With pocket knife, cut three narrow sticks from shingle, lengthwise. Sand sticks until they are the same thickness. Cut one stick so that it is ⅔ the length of the long ones.

2. Make an **X** with the two long sticks and lay the third one horizontally over them. Bind the three sticks together with kite string.

You will need: 1 cedar shingle   Glue
Tissue paper   Rags
Scissors   Pocket knife
Kite string   Sand paper

3. Slit all three sticks at each end. Run piece of string through slits and all around kite. Secure string at each slit and tie it tight at starting point. Lay kite frame on piece of wrapping paper. Trim paper 1″ larger than frame all the way around. Cut notches in corners to make flaps. Fold and glue each flap over string.

4. Tie loop of string to bottom ends of long sticks and tie a kite tail of knotted rags to it. On front side, tie loop of string to each stick from one end to other. Keep them loose enough to cross in middle a few inches in front of kite's face. Tie remaining kite string to center point of these three strings and kite is ready to fly.

161

Wind Streamers

1 2" x 4' strip of newsprint, newspaper, or crepe paper per child.

This activity should be done on a day when wind is blowing. A discussion of wind may be held first. Some questions to ask: Can the wind be seen? How do you know when the wind is blowing? Can what the wind does be seen? Can the wind be felt? Give each child a streamer to take outside. Allow the children to make observations of what happens to the streamers when they stand still, run, or walk; what happens to the streamers when the wind blows hard. The children will also enjoy making patterns with the streamers.

Making Rainbows

You will need: *1 prism*

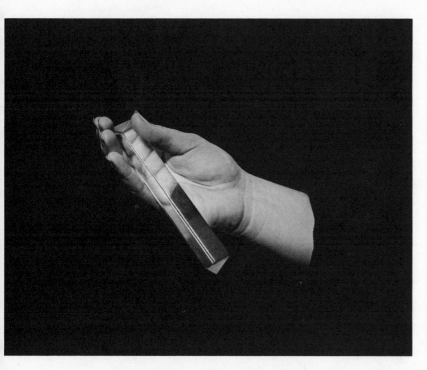

1. To see how April showers make rainbows, darken room to be used. Hold prism in ray of sunlight. By rotating prism, all the colors will appear on darkened area of the room. Sunlight is made up of seven colors: red, orange, yellow, green, blue, indigo and violet. When the sunlight travels through a prism or through rain drops, its rays are bent, separating the colors.

2. Close drapes of room, allowing only a small ray of sunlight to come through. Place a table where sunlight hits. On the table put a dish of water so sun shines directly on it. Place edge of mirror in water so that a rainbow appears on wall or ceiling.

Sweetheart Soap

You will need:

1 *cup soap flakes*
½ *cup water*
   Few drops of food coloring
   Milk carton or metal cookie cutters
   Wax paper
   Bowl
   Saucepan and potholder
   Spatula
   Eggbeater

If using milk carton, cut it into 1″ strips and bend into desirable shapes such as hearts, flowers, moon, etc. Staple ends together. Place these molds on wax paper. Boil water and pour it over soapflakes in bowl. Stir with spatula until soapflakes are dissolved. Beat mixture with eggbeater until satiny, like taffy. Stir in food coloring if desired. Fill molds with soap mixture and let dry for two days before removing.

Bath Salts

You will need:

1 cup Epsom salt
28 drops food coloring (any color)
1 large jar with lid
1 ornamental jar

Combine Epsom salt and food coloring in one of the jars and shake until color has spread. Pour these bath salts into ornamental jar for mother. Add a pinch of bath salts to every bath. The food coloring used will not change color or harm the body. Two-color salts may be made and layered in jar for a pretty gift.

Garden-Fresh Hand Lotion

You will need: *1 cucumber, several drops of lemon extract, bowl, cheesecloth, grater, spoon, tiny jar with lid*

1. Line bowl with cheesecloth so edges overhang. Wash cucumber and grate into cloth. Bring corners of cloth together and twist cloth until pulp is pressed into a ball. Continue wringing until all juice is squeezed into bowl. Throw pulp away.

2. Stir several drops of lemon extract into cucumber juice. The hand lotion is ready to use. Spoon it into a covered jar, and it will stay fresh in refrigerator for 3 to 4 days.

Flower Fragrance Perfume

You will need:

1 cup fragrant flowers—roses, violets, lilacs
1 cup water
Bowl
Cheesecloth
Saucepan
Potholders
Funnel
Tiny jar with lid

Line inside of bowl with cloth so edges overhang. Tear enough flower petals into small pieces to measure 1 cup, and place into cloth. Boil the water and pour over petals until they are covered. Let soak overnight. The next day gather corners of the cloth together and wring out all liquid. Discard petals. Put scented water into saucepan and boil until there is one tablespoon left. Pour perfume through funnel into bottle. Cover tightly. The perfume is ready to wear and will last a month.

Mother's Day Bulletin Board

Have the children draw portraits of their mothers. Mount these on construction paper on the bulletin board. These later can be taken home as Mother's Day cards.

You will need:

Construction paper
Crayons or markers

Soap on a Rope

You will need:

1 cup soap flakes
½ cup water
1 yard cotton rope
  Few drops of food coloring
  Small gelatin molds
  Bowl
  Pan
  Spatula
  Eggbeater

Boil the water and pour it over soap flakes and food coloring in bowl. Stir with spatula until soapflakes are dissolved. Use eggbeater to whip mixture until it is satiny, like taffy. Fill gelatin molds and insert a cotton rope into middle of soap. Let soap dry two days before removing molds.

Father's Day Card

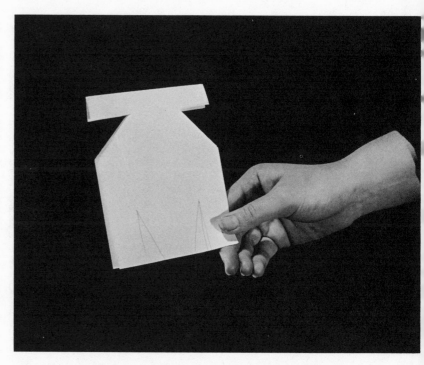

1. Fold piece of paper lengthwise so it measures 4¼″ x 11″. Place fold on left side. Fold top to meet bottom, making a 4¼″ x 5½″ rectangle. Keep this fold on top.

2. ¾″ down from top fold on right and left sides make a 1¼″ cut towards middle. On outside edges, measure down 1½″ from these cuts. Cut from this point to ends of first cuts.

You will need: *1 8½″ x 11″ piece of white paper*
Scissors
Ruler
Marking pen

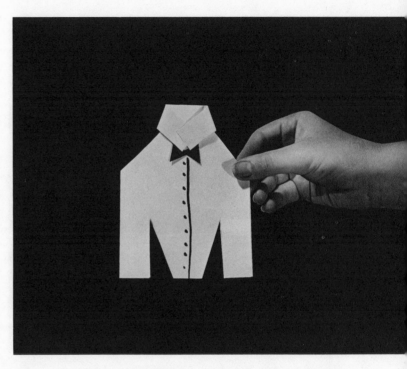

3. On bottom measure 1″ and 1¾″ towards middle from each side. At 1″ point, cut up 2″. From 1¾″ points, cut diagonally up to end of 2″ cuts.

4. Fold top pieces in to resemble a collar on a shirt. Draw on buttons and tie. Open card up to write a Father's Day message inside.

Pants Hanger for Dad

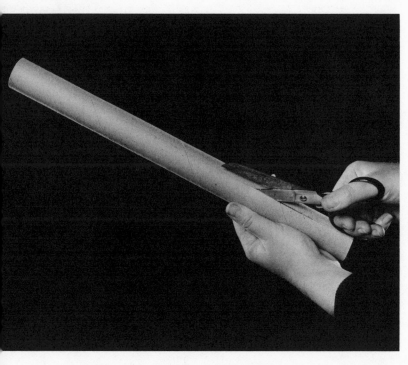

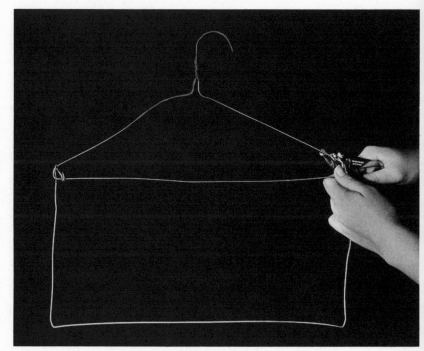

1. Cut the tubes open from one end to the other.

2. With pliers, open one clothes hanger and cut off curved part of hanger. Open hanger up and attach to good hanger by twisting ends in place.

You will need: 3 *paper towel tubes*   *Scissors*
                    2 *wire hangers*   *Tape*
                        Rug yarn   *Pliers*

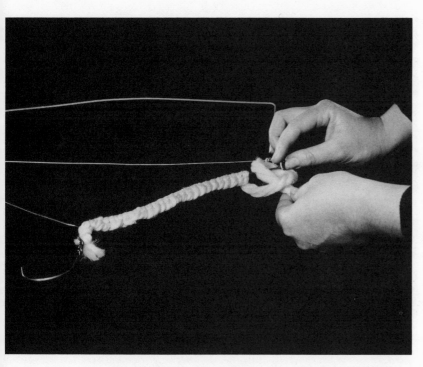

3. Cover top and sides of hanger with yarn, wrapping with half-hitch knots, as shown.

4. Place tubes over bottoms of hangers and tape in place. Wind yarn around and secure. This hanger will hold two pairs of pants.

Rag Bags

 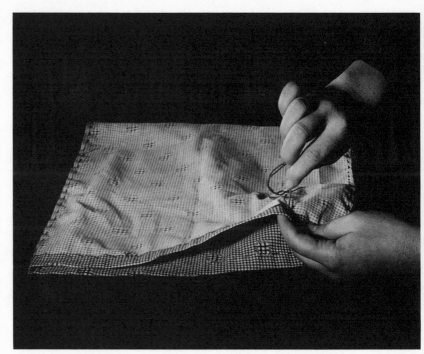

1. Fold piece of fabric in half, wrong sides together, to make a 14″ x 14″ square. Iron it flat. Sew up the sides, leaving top open.

2. Fold top edge down ½″ and press with iron. Sew this as close to raw edge as possible.

You will need: 1 14″ x 28″ piece of fabric   Iron
            2 36″ shoelaces   Scissors
                 Sewing machine, needle and   Several large scraps of soft
                     thread, or glue   material for rags

3. From right side of fabric, open a ¼″ slit in top hem near each side seam. Reinforce ends of slits with several stitches. Insert one shoelace through one slit and pull completely around so both ends of shoelace can be tied together. Repeat with other shoelace at opposite opening.

4. Place scraps of material inside the rag bag. Dad can use these in his car, in his workshop, or around the house.

Father's Day Bulletin Board

Have the children draw pictures of things their fathers do. Mount them on construction paper on the bulletin board.

You will need:

Paper
Crayons or marking pens

Flag Day Fantasy

Have the children create their own designs for the first flag of the United States. Use these pictures for a bulletin board or scrapbook.

You will need:

Paper
Crayons, felt tip markers, or paint
Fabric scraps
Glue
Scissors

Uncle Sam Hat

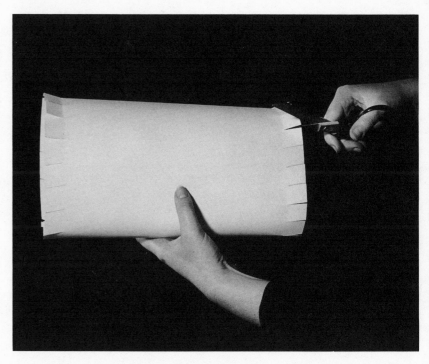

1. Cut a 12″ circle from the white construction paper. Cut a 6″ circle from the center of the 12″ circle. The 12″ circle becomes the brim and the 6″ circle the top of the hat.

2. From another piece of white paper roll up a cylinder to fit the brim of the hat. Make ½″ slits around the top and bottom of the cylinder.

178

You will need: *Red, white, and blue construction paper*
                            Scissors
                            Glue

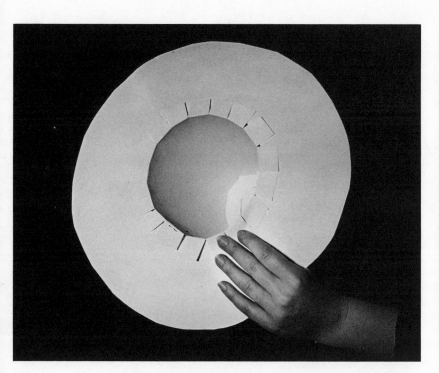

3. Fold one end of the cylinder out from the slits and glue onto the bottom side of the brim. Fold the cylinder in at the other end and glue to the top of the hat.

4. Glue a 3″ blue band around the bottom of the cylinder. Glue white stars on top of this. Cut 1″ red strips and glue up and down the cylinder, leaving some white between them. The hat is ready to wear.

179

Fourth of July Patriotic Cake

Cake:
    ½ cup butter
    ½ cup margarine
    2 cups sugar
    3 cups sifted cake flour
    4 teaspoons baking powder
    1 teaspoon salt
    1 cup non-fat milk
    ⅓ cup water
    6 egg whites, stiffly beaten
Frosting:
    2 egg whites
    1 cup sugar
    ⅛ teaspoon cream of tartar
    ¼ cup water
    1 teaspoon vanilla

Cream together butter, margarine, and sugar until fluffy. Sift dry ingredients together and add alternately with milk, water, and vanilla. Fold in egg whites. Divide dough into three portions. With food coloring, make one portion red, one blue, and leave third plain. Bake each portion in its own greased and floured 8″ cake pan in 350° oven for 35 minutes. Cool before frosting. Fill cake layers with real whipped cream or vanilla custard. To make frosting, combine egg whites, sugar, cream of tartar and water in top of double boiler. Place over boiling water and beat 7 minutes. Fold in vanilla. Spread over cake and decorate with candy or jellies. Top cake with sparklers and candles before serving.

Making Raisins

You will need:

1 *bunch firm Thompson seedless grapes*
Large pan of water
Plastic coated trays or paper plates
Pieces of clean cheesecloth, mosquito
  netting, or wire screen, large enough
  to cover trays
Glass jar with lid

Wash grapes thoroughly and blot dry with towel. Remove grapes from stem and spread on tray. Cover grapes and tray securely with cloth or screen to keep off insects and dirt. Place tray of grapes in direct sunlight, making sure air can circulate freely over and under tray. After 4 days, test grapes for dryness. Squeeze a grape in the hand; if there is no moisture, the raisins are done. If not, keep them in sun and check every day until ready. The raisins should be pliable and leathery. Store in an airtight container in a cool place and they should remain in prime condition for six months. It is interesting to weigh the grapes before drying them and record the weight; then weigh the raisins and compare the difference.

181

Fruit Leather

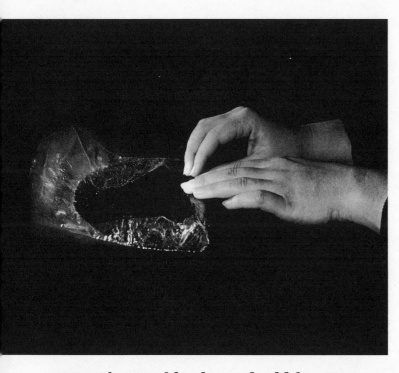

You will need:

Blender
Honey
Plastic wrap
Choice of one or more of these fruits: apricot, peach, nectarines, berry, pear, prune, apple, apple and pineapple or bananas.

Puree fruit in blender and add honey to taste, if desired. Pour out on lightly oiled cookie sheet or onto plastic wrap which has been secured to cookie sheet with tape. The mixture should be ¼″ thick on cookie sheet. Dry fruit leather in a dehydrator, an oven, or in the sun. Turn oven to 200°, leaving door ajar. Place sheet in center of oven and turn it from front to back occasionally. This process will take 4–6 hours. Pull off fruit leather while still warm and place on plastic wrap. Roll it up, paper and all, and store in an airtight container.

Apple Harvest

You will need:

*Several apples of different varieties,
  sliced*
Applesauce:
  10 pippin apples
  2½ cups water
  ¾ cup brown sugar
  ½ teaspoon cinnamon

1. September is a good time to visit apple orchards and observe harvesting. Bring several apples of different varieties to classroom and let the children examine and taste the apples. See if they can note differences in taste among the apples.

2. Have children prepare applesauce by peeling, coring, and slicing apples in small pieces. Place apples, water, and brown sugar into bowl and mix. Sprinkle with cinnamon. Pour ingredients into hot frying pan. Take turns stirring apples until soft, about 15 minutes. Mash any whole pieces of apple that are left. When cool, applesauce is ready to eat.

183

Columbus Day Compass

You will need:

1 *small bowl of water*
1 *magnet*
1 *needle*
1 *cork*

Rub the magnet over the needle 50 times in the same direction to magnetize the needle. Put the needle into the cork and place into the bowl of water. Turn the cork in many directions and let it go. It will always come to rest pointing north.

Santa Maria Pizza

You will need:

Large mixing bowl
Large frying pan
Spoon
Breadboard
Cookie sheet

Pizza dough:
  1 cup warm water (105°–115° F.)
  1 package active dry yeast
  1 tablespoon salad oil
  1 teaspoon honey
  1 teaspoon salt
  2½ cups whole wheat flour

Pizza sauce:
  1½ lbs ground beef
  2 chopped onions
  2 cloves of garlic
  1 16-oz. can tomato sauce
  1 35-oz. can whole tomatoes
  1 teaspoon salt
  ½ teaspoon oregano
  ½ teaspoon basil
  ½ pound mozzarella cheese
  ¾ cup Parmesan cheese

Make dough first. Mix warm water, yeast, salad oil, honey, and salt together in bowl and let stand 5 minutes. Add whole wheat flour and mix well. Shape dough into ball and place in oiled bowl, turning dough to grease surface. Let dough rise in warm place for 45 minutes. Start sauce in large frying pan. Add ground beef, chopped onions, and minced garlic. Cook and stir often until meat is brown. Add tomato sauce, drained whole tomatoes, salt, oregano and basil. Stir until tomatoes are broken into small pieces. Cook over medium heat about 15 minutes. Stir occasionally. When dough has risen, punch it down with your fist. Preheat oven to 475°. Knead dough on floured board until smooth. Add more flour if too sticky. Divide dough into two parts (or give each child his own portion). Cover each cookie sheet with dough if making two large pizzas. Cover dough with sauce; add thinly sliced mozzarella cheese and then Parmesan cheese. Bake pizza on bottom rack of oven for 25 minutes until crust is brown and cheese melted.

Grinding Wheat

1. Autumn is the time to harvest and grind grains. Put the kernels of wheat into the wheat grinder. Sift the ground wheat and use the coarse part for cereal and the flour for the bread.

You will need: *Kernels of wheat*   *2 mixing bowls*
Wheat grinder   *Wooden spoon*
Sifter   *Saucepan*
Baking sheets or loaf pans

Ingredients for bread:
    3 cups whole wheat flour
    1 cup milk
    1 package active dry yeast
    ¼ cup brown sugar or molasses
    2 teaspoons salt
    ½ cup boiling water

2. To make bread, put the package of yeast into a mixing bowl with ½ cup warm water (105°–115° F.). Let stand 5 minutes. Put into a separate bowl: 1 cup milk, ½ cup boiling water, ¼ cup molasses, and 2 teaspoons of salt. Mix well and cool to lukewarm. Add to the yeast mixture. Stir in 3 cups of flour with the hands or a heavy spoon. If it is too sticky, add more flour. Knead this until it is smooth. Let it rise until it doubles in size (about 1 hour). Shape into loaves and place in lightly greased pans or roll into rolls and place on lightly greased baking sheets. Bake at 375° until golden brown and loaves sound hollow when tapped. Bake the loaves about 50 minutes and the rolls about 20–30 minutes.

Cooking for the Birds

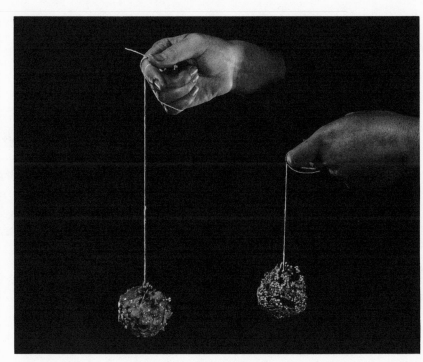

1. Make a Christmas tree for a bird by decorating a bush or tree with strings of popcorn, seeds, fruits, coconut pieces and other goodies from the list above.

2. Bird pudding is made by mixing ½ pound of lard, 1 cup peanut butter, and enough oatmeal to hold the mixture together without making it too dry. Roll pine cones into this mixture, attach a string from the top, and hang it from a tree.

You will need:

Popcorn	Slices of oranges or	Oatmeal
Sunflower or	grapefruit	Bird seed
pumpkin seeds	Bread	Peanut butter
Coconut pieces	Chunks of suet	String
Berries	Lard	Needle

Variation: Pine cones can also be rolled in plain peanut butter, then rolled into bird seed and hung from trees.

Bird Feeders

Orange or Onion Bag

Plastic Milk Bottle Feeder

You will need: *10" x 10" piece of a mesh onion or orange bag, string, lard or suet*

Place the suet inside the orange bag and tie it shut with the string. Hang this from a tree.

You will need: *Plastic milk or punch bottle, knife, string, bird seed*

Cut a 2" wide slit around the front and halfway around each side. Fill the bottom with bird seed. Attach a string around the handle and hang from a tree.

Lid and Doughnut Hanger

Coconut Hanger

You will need: *2 identical jar lids, large nail, stale plain doughnut, string, hammer*

Hammer nail through middle of both lids. Remove nail from lids. Put nail through hole of one lid, hole of doughnut and through hole of other lid. Cover top of nail with masking tape. Tie string on nail and hang from a tree.

You will need: *Half a coconut shell; bird seed, berries, or fruit seeds; 4 36″ pieces of heavy string*

Knot or weave strings together at midpoint and place them on bottom of coconut shell. Bring up ends and knot them together over the coconut shell. Fill shell with bird food and hang from a tree.